Th

·BRITAIN·
A COUNTRY REVEALED

·BRITAIN·

A COUNTRY REVEALED

Produced by AA Publishing
Copyright © AA Media Limited 2006
Reprinted 2009
New edition, revised and updated 2010

Written by Sally Roy
Revised and updated by Tim Locke

Edited by David Popey
Design by Austin Taylor
Picture research by Ian Little
Proofreading by Pam Stagg
Internal repro and image manipulation by Sarah Montgomery
Indexing by Marie Lorimer

ISBN 978 0 7495 6735 4

Published by AA Publishing (a trading name of AA Media Limited,
whose registered office is Fanum House, Basing View, Basingstoke,
Hampshire RG21 4EA; registered number 06112600).

A04451

Printed in China by C&C Offset Printing Co., Ltd

Visit AA Publishing at theAA.com/shop

PAGE 1 *Rowing boats moored on the River Wear near Elvet Bridge, Durham*
PAGE 2 *A rocky shoreline on the Isle of Skye*
PAGE 3 *The remains of Wheal Betsy Tin Mine, Dartmoor National Park*
PAGES 4–5 *Cwm Prysor Valley, Snowdonia National Park*

Contents

London

The capital of Britain, a vast metropolis stretching more than 30 miles (48km) to the north and south of the River Thames, London is Europe's largest and ethnically most diverse city. It dominates British national life, is the centre of law-making and the hub of the money markets. Its citizens see themselves as a people apart, with provincial life beginning where the city ends. Londoners have every reason to be proud of their city, an exciting and dynamic urban sprawl, whose confines contain world-class museums and galleries, historic buildings, magnificent churches and cathedrals, huge and verdant parks and gardens, and some of the best theatre, music, shopping and eating to be found anywhere in the world.

The city was founded as the capital of Roman Britain in AD43, but its main expansion started after the Norman Conquest of 1066, when William of Normandy was crowned king in Westminster Abbey, and has continued ever since. Over the centuries, London has spread to absorb scores of villages that once stood well outside its walls, and that now form the wonderfully varied neighbourhoods of this culturally rich city.

Many districts are inhabited by descendants of the immigrants who have poured into London through the ages – in the last century alone, thousands arrived from the Caribbean, the Indian subcontinent, the Mediterranean and the Far East. Today, like the native Cockneys from the working-class inner districts and Britons from all over the country who work here, they see themselves as Londoners, with a sense of historical and cultural pride in their unmatched city.

Tower Bridge, London's iconic gateway on the River Thames since 1894, is both a swing and bascule bridge that is lifted around 1,000 times a year

Trafalgar Square

From Parliament and the neighbouring Westminster Abbey – scene of every English coronation since the 11th century – Whitehall runs north to Trafalgar Square, designed by Charles Barry and John Nash and built between 1829 and 1841 to commemorate Admiral Lord Nelson and his 1805 victory against the French at Trafalgar. Surrounded by fountains and guarded by sculptural lions, a statue of the great man stands atop a 165 feet (50m) column, gazing benignly over the political demonstrations and public celebrations the square hosts each year.

LEFT Trafalgar Square is one of the few London streetscapes with fountains. They are overlooked by the church of St-Martin-in-the-Fields, noted for its tradition of church and chamber music, and its care for homeless people

The Houses of Parliament

Britain's laws have been debated at the Westminster parliament since the 16th century. Members meet in two chambers in the grandiose riverside building designed by Charles Barry and Augustus Pugin, after a fire in 1834 destroyed much of the older structure. The superb Westminster Hall, built in 1199 and topped by Europe's largest hammerbeam roof, survived this fire, and is still used as a place of lying-in-state for monarchs and their consorts. For many visitors Parliament is synonymous with the 1859 clock tower, known as 'Big Ben' after the giant bell inside.

ABOVE Behind the riverside terrace of the Houses of Parliament lie the debating chambers, flanked by 'Big Ben' on the right. The Commons chamber, dating from 1858, was rebuilt after its destruction by bombing during the Second World War

Tate Modern

South across the river, and reached on foot via the stylish Millennium Bridge, there's art of a very different kind at Tate Modern, where a vast international collection of 20th- and 21st-century artworks is housed in the former Bankside Power Station. Tate Modern is the largest modern art gallery in the world, including works by artists as diverse as Picasso, Dalí and Rothko. Works are displayed thematically rather than chronologically, giving a thought-provoking edge to the displays that's missing in many of London's older galleries.

The building itself is a brilliant conversion of an industrial space, which has retained the sober atmosphere of the massive turbine hall, mainly used for cutting-edge installation art, while providing wonderfully light and spacious galleries on the upper floors, and sweeping views of the city from its bar on the top floor.

St Paul's Cathedral

In 1666, the Great Fire swept through the City of London, destroying acres of buildings, among them old St Paul's Cathedral. Architect Christopher Wren was commissioned to design a new one, along with 51 other City churches, and work started in 1675, continuing until 1711.

Distinctly baroque in spirit, the cathedral is surmounted by a massive classical dome, and fronted by two towers which flank the classically inspired entrance with its pediment and pilasters. Inside, this architectural set piece is lavishly decorated with intricately carved wood, marble and gilding, seen at its best in the chancel and choir. Overhead soars the great dome, encircled by the Whispering Gallery, so called because of its acoustic properties – words whispered on one side are audible over 100 feet (30m) away on the other.

The nave is packed with monuments to the great, including an effigy of the metaphysical poet John Donne (*c*.1572–1631), one-time dean of St Paul's. There are more star names in the crypt, burial place of Nelson, Wellington and Wren himself, whose modest tomb is carved with a Latin inscription that translates as 'Reader, if you seek his memorial, look about you'.

LEFT *Tate Modern, formerly the Bankside Power Station, as seen from beneath the Millennium Bridge, which in 2000 was the first span to be built over the Thames in 106 years*

RIGHT *Trompe l'oeil frescoes by James Thornhill decorate the inner dome of St Paul's Cathedral, high above Grinling Gibbons' carved choir stalls. He also created the superb organ case carving; the instrument has been played by Handel and Mendelssohn*

New London Landmarks

London acquired a whole new set of striking structures for the Millennium, most notably the London Eye, a giant observation wheel on the south bank of the Thames. Designed by the architects Julia Barfield and David Marks, the wheel, 443 feet (135m) high, is the largest ever to be built, its 32 constantly moving capsules giving ever-widening views over London as they slowly rise and fall. The Eye has quickly proved itself both a favourite London landmark and one of the capital's most popular attractions. More than 10,000 people daily take a half-hour 'flight', which offers the unique experience of seeing the whole city. Further downstream, one of the latest additions to the skyline is the precipitously pointed 'Shard' complex, intended to bring some glitz to the Borough area around London Bridge station and will be Britain's tallest building at an estimated height of 1,017 feet (310m).

Across the Thames to the northeast rise more 21st-century architectural splendours – great towers of glass and steel, which celebrate London's status as one of the world's premier financial centres. Among the most revolutionary is the Swiss Re Tower, affectionately dubbed the Gherkin by Londoners even before its completion in 2004. Designed by Norman Foster, the building features a giant atria and a double-glazed exterior, made almost entirely of flat panes of glass, that helps control the temperature of the interior and reduces energy use.

The use of glass and steel, are hallmarks of Foster and Partners' work, which can also be seen at the bulbous glass City Hall (Greater London Authority headquarters) across the river in Southwark, at the J Sainsbury headquarters on Holborn Circus and at 8 Canada Square (also known as the HSBC Tower) in the London Docklands.

London's Markets

The ethnic melting pot that London became during the 20th century brought an influx of food and goods from all over the world, and the city's markets are a spectacle in themselves, as much as of the traders and shoppers as the vast range of what is on sale.

Since the Middle Ages, London's wholesale markets – Smithfield for meat, Billingsgate for fish, and Covent Garden for fruit and vegetables – have supplied the city's needs in a frenzy of dawn activity laced with Cockney charm, which continues today. Covent Garden moved to an unglamorous site at Nine Elms south of the river in 1974, but Smithfield, whose prices affect meat and poultry

BELOW *Once London's wholesale fresh produce market, the glass-roofed former Covent Garden building is now home to chic boutiques and craft stalls, and a venue for street entertainers. The produce market moved to a new site, 3 miles (5km) away in Nine Elms, and became known as New Covent Garden Market*

RIGHT *Tucked away in the streets behind Covent Garden piazza, tiny Neal's Yard is one of the best places to track down food specialities such as good breads and cheeses, or relax with a freshly ground coffee*

costs throughout the UK, and Billingsgate, shifting 25,000 tonnes of fish annually, still occupy fine purpose-built Victorian buildings in east London.

Londoners are discerning food shoppers, and there's been a big revival in retail market shopping, with Leadenhall in the City and Borough Market in Southwark topping the list in terms of choice and quality. Elsewhere, street markets combine food stalls with clothes, arts and crafts and antiques. Camden is the biggest and best, but Petticoat Lane in the east, Portobello Road, just off trendy Notting Hill, Spitalfields, once home to Huguenot silk-weavers, and Bermondsey all have their fans, while shoppers with a real appreciation of cultural diversity head straight for Brick Lane.

RIGHT *Portobello Road in Notting Hill boasts the world's largest antiques market, a fascinating browsing ground for all manner of items such as barometers, clothing, vintage cameras, silverware, porcelain and antique toys*

BELOW *Borough Market, on the same site since 1755 and housed in an imposing Victorian structure, has become the capital's leading produce market, much favoured by restaurateurs*

Buckingham Palace

Buckingham Palace, the Queen's official residence, was originally built in 1702 as the Duke of Buckingham's city house. In 1762 it was sold to George III as a private dwelling for Queen Charlotte. During the 1820s it was enlarged according to designs by John Nash, becoming the monarch's official London residence with the accession of Queen Victoria in 1837. More alterations in 1913 produced today's building, a 300-room colossus whose sumptuous state rooms are open to the public during the summer.

The Palace stands at the head of the Mall, an arrow-straight, tree-lined avenue which skirts St James' Park, the oldest of the royal parks, and leads down to Trafalgar Square via the grandiose Admiralty Arch. On state occasions the Mall is the route of all ceremonial processions, an aspect of British life that enthrals tourists and brings a swell of pride to Londoners, who believe – with some justification – that no other nation puts on such a good a show of pageantry as the British.

The hallmarks of the big occasions are immaculate marching, brass bands, colourful military uniforms and gleaming horses. Many of these elements can be enjoyed on a daily basis at the ceremony of the Changing of the Guard outside Buckingham Palace, when a detachment of the Queen's Foot Guards marches up the Mall to replace the outgoing guard at the entrance to the Palace.

RIGHT Guardsmen parading in front of Buckingham Palace are a frequent sight. They wear ceremonial tall fur caps known as bearskins, a tradition dating from the Battle of Waterloo

BELOW Serried ranks of spring planting flank the Victoria Memorial in front of Buckingham Palace. The monument was erected by Edward VII in tribute to his late mother

Southeast England

This corner of England has long been under pressure from London; beyond the Green Belt – a protected swathe of countryside that rings the capital – spread the densely populated counties of Surrey, Hampshire, Kent and Sussex. Despite the pressures of population, the southeast has retained glorious countryside, historic towns and some superbly unspoiled stretches of coastline, all of which provide escape and recreation for the millions of people living in, or on the fringes of, the capital.

Along this coastline are sited the main Channel ports of Dover and Folkestone, Ramsgate and Deal, their history bound up with the story of threats of invasion over the centuries. The Romans invaded here in 43AD, William the Conqueror won England in a battle just outside Hastings in 1066, and during the Second World War, the skies over Kent were the scene of the Battle of Britain. The towns and cities of this region are rich in history, from Canterbury, where Christianity was first re-established after Roman times, to Portsmouth, home to the Royal Navy, and Windsor, its castle a mighty expression of royal power.

Away from the holiday bustle of its seaside resorts, the southeast has hung on to great stretches of untouched and protected landscape. These include the great walking country of the Weald, with its attractive old villages and hedge-lined pastures, and the chalky heights of the South Downs, and the rolling woods and heathland of the New Forest, where, a short walk from the car parks, there's utter peace and an abundance of wildlife.

Ponies roam freely on the heathlands of the New Forest. They are not wild, but are owned by commoners who have long-held grazing rights

The Sussex Coastline

ABOVE *Low tide leaves a complex of rock pools, teeming with marine life, on the beach beneath the white chalk cliffs of the Seven Sisters*

OPPOSITE *The first lighthouse on Beachy Head was built in 1702. This one, at the foot of the receding cliffs, dates from 1902*

Between Seaford and Eastbourne the coastline rises to the spectacular cliffs of Beachy Head. Here, where the South Downs meet the sea, vast cliffs of pure white chalk rise to a height, at the headland, of 536 feet (163m).

There's no beach below – the name comes from the Norman French words *beau chef*, meaning 'beautiful head', and Britain's highest chalk sea cliff is certainly that, with panoramas east to Dungeness in Kent and west into West Sussex. Its startling whiteness is due to the constant process of erosion along this stretch of coast. The sea gnawing at the base of the cliffs causes regular landfalls, which expose new layers of clean chalk, and as a result the cliffs are receding at about 12 inches (30cm) each year.

This process continues along the neighbouring cliffs of the Sussex Heritage Coast, a stretch of sharp rises and dips known as the Seven Sisters. A footpath, the eastern end of the South Downs Way (100 miles/161km), runs along the clifftops providing one of the most exhilarating and impressive walks in the region. The track finally drops down into the valley of the River Cuckmere and follows it inland to Alfriston, a beguiling village whose 14th-century parish church is known as the 'Cathedral of the Downs'.

Dover

ABOVE *The walls and keep of Dover Castle, which today sit high above the busy European ferry terminal, enclose a Roman pharos (lighthouse) and a 7th-century Saxon church*

The White Cliffs of Dover, for centuries the first or last sight of England for many travellers, majestically flank one of Britain's major sea ports. The Romans saw the defensive potential and chose this coastal point as the base for their northern fleet, building a lighthouse to guide in their ships. That lighthouse is now enclosed by the massive fortifications of Dover Castle, constructed in 1168 by the Normans and used as a military installation throughout every major European conflict involving Britain up until the mid-20th century.

Beneath the keep, cut into the cliffs, is a warren of tunnels which were excavated during the Napoleonic Wars. They found another purpose during the Second World War, when they were used as the planning headquarters for the evacuation of Allied troops from the beaches of Dunkirk. Today the tunnels are a major tourist attraction.

Canterbury

In medieval times, Dover was the entry port for thousands of pilgrims en route to the famous shrine of the martyr St Thomas à Becket at Canterbury, some 16 miles (26km) inland to the north. It was a pilgrimage celebrated by the poet Geoffrey Chaucer in his greatest work, *The Canterbury Tales* of c.1390.

Historic Canterbury is still partly ringed by ancient defensive walls. Its fine cathedral, which incorporates an original Norman crypt, is the mother church of the Church of England. This was the scene, in 1170, of the murder of the Archbishop Thomas à Becket on the orders of Henry II. Nearby are the scant ruins of England's first Christian complex – an abbey founded by St Augustine in AD598, and St Martin's, the oldest church in the English-speaking world, where King Ethelbert was baptised in AD597.

ABOVE *The wealth of magnificent medieval and later stained-glass windows within the cathedral include this one commemorating the murder of Thomas à Becket*

RIGHT *Canterbury Cathedral features a magnificent central tower known as Bell Harry, built between 1490 and 1510. Just before 9pm, a bell within strikes a hundred times to signal a daily curfew*

Royal Ascot

In 1711, while riding out from Windsor, Queen Anne came across a patch of open heathland that seemed an ideal place for 'horses to gallop at full stretch'. The area was called East Cote, and by August of that year a course had been built and Royal Ascot was born. There were one or two setbacks to the growth of Ascot's popularity – George I was totally uninterested in racing – but by 1760 Ascot was established as a focal point of fashion for anyone passionate about the sport. In 1790, George III had a temporary stand erected for himself and his guests; this was the first Royal Enclosure, accessible only by royal invitation, and today it's the area from which the royal family and thousands of patrons watch the meeting.

BELOW *The Gold Cup meeting on the third day is known as Ladies' Day, when ladies show off their fashions – particularly their hats*

Every monarch since the time of George III has come racing during Ascot Week, whose pattern, since the early 20th century, follows a strict timetable. The Queen and the Duke of Edinburgh attend every day of the five-day meeting held in mid-June, driving from Windsor Castle and processing down the course to the royal box in open landaus, accompanied by their guests. The Queen is a passionate horsewoman and owner, who has had many wins at Ascot over the years.

For many race goers, though, horses come a poor second place to fashion and fun, for Ascot, of all British race meetings, provides a glorious excuse to dress up, particularly on the Thursday of Ascot Week: Ladies' Day.

ABOVE *Races at Ascot are held at various points in the year. Brightly coloured silks worn by the jockeys make identification easy as the field of horses thunder down the course*

RIGHT *Each day of the week of Royal Ascot races, the Queen and the Duke of Edinburgh head a carriage procession along the course*

Bodiam Castle

From the time of the Norman invasion in 1066, the English aristocracy built themselves fortified castles, both as places of refuge and as grandiose statements of their power and wealth. Many still survive, and through them can be traced the evolution of castles, from defensive strongholds to huge mansions designed for luxurious living.

The southeast is rich in such castles, some virtually unchanged since medieval times, others that have been refashioned over the centuries as needs and fashion dictated. Early castles had the additional protection of a moat, and few are more impressive than Bodiam in East Sussex. It was built in 1385 as a refuge from French invaders and stands as a perfect example of a medieval castle, with towers and battlements reflected in the surrounding waters. Despite a skirmish in 1483, its defensive powers were never really tested.

Rye

An attractive mix of half-timbered and tile-hung Tudor brick cottages, imposing Georgian houses and cobbled streets, the ancient town of Rye perches on a sandstone hill above the River Rother and the expanse of the Romney Marshes.

In the Middle Ages, Rye was an important port and a proud member of the confederation of the Cinque Ports, established to provide the monarch with maritime support in return for trading privileges. By the 18th century, these rights were interpreted by local sailors as a licence for large-scale smuggling, viewed by the townspeople as a perfectly legitimate trade, and many of Rye's finest houses were built with the ill-gotten profits.

Today Rye's sea harbour is gone, the river is silted up and the town now lies peacefully marooned 2 miles (3km) inland. It remains a prosperous market centre, whose myriad weekend visitors come to stroll along the picturesque lanes and through the formidably fortified Land Gate, browse in the antiques shops and galleries, and take in the Ypres Tower, once used as a lookout point for cross-Channel invaders.

Rye hosts an annual Arts Festival each September, which includes music and literature. It is a fitting event for a town, which numbers writers such as Henry James and E F Benson among its former citizens.

ABOVE *Sloping Mermaid Street contains some of Rye's most venerable buildings, such as the timber-framed 16th-century Old Hospital and Lamb House, once home to American novelist Henry James*

LEFT *Rye's windmill replaced an earlier, 16th-century version in 1932, and housed a bakery and pottery before becoming a well-known guest house*

29

Brighton

Brash, buzzy Brighton is the southeast's major resort. It set the trend for seaside frolics back in the 1780s, when the Prince of Wales (the future George IV) took up the newly fashionable pastime of sea bathing and came to the modest fishing town of Brighthelmstone with his mistress, Mrs Fitzherbert.

As Prince Regent after 1810, he had the money (and the authority) to build himself a pleasure palace, the extraordinary Royal Pavilion, whose flamboyant architecture earned it its own sobriquet: Oriental-Gothic. All Indian- and Chinese-inspired domes and minarets outside, the Pavilion's interior, complete with chandeliers, glittering cupolas and a vast banqueting hall, set the standard for what was to become the effervescent sense of fun that is the town's hallmark.

Thousands of London day-trippers, liberated by the railways, poured here in the 19th century, and it was for their amusement that three piers were built, one of which, Brighton Pier, is still functioning today. Modern Brighton, with its Georgian houses, and classy antiques shops and smart restaurants in the warren of old streets known as The Lanes, tries hard to sell itself as a middle-class town, but the big student presence, the free-spending weekenders and Britain's most thriving gay community ensure that it will always remain unmistakably vibrant, fun-loving and sophisticated.

BELOW *Brighton has for long been a place of pleasure and fun, and is full of period charm. This Victorian merry-go-round stands on the beach close to Brighton Pier*

ABOVE *The Peace Statue marks the border between Brighton and Hove and was erected in 1912, in memory of Edward VII*

RIGHT *Installed by the beach and titled* Afloat, *this 1998 doughnut-shaped bronze sculpture by Hamish Black represents a globe, with the North and South Poles pushed together to form the central hole*

OVER *The architect John Nash was responsible for transforming a simple Georgian farmhouse into the exuberant Royal Pavilion in 1815 that put Brighton at the height of fashion*

MAX MILLER
1894 — 1963

"The Pure Gold of The Music Hall"

ABOVE *The Lanes, an intricate knot of little streets and alleys, close to the seafront, is packed with restaurants, boutiques and jewellery shops*

BELOW *Brighton station acquired its ornate clock in the 19th century, when thousands of London workers came by train for a taste of the pleasures of the seaside*

ABOVE *Brighton's history as a place of fun-seeking is highlighted by this statue of the legendary former resident and music hall comedy artist Max Miller, outside the Brighton Dome concert hall*

INSIDE *Piers, with their promenades and amusements, were a unique element of the development of English holiday resorts. Brighton Pier, originally the Palace Pier, was built in 1899 and remains the centre of the resort's traditional seaside amusements*

Knebworth

By Tudor times, the building style favoured by the wealthy and powerful was changing. In Hertfordshire in 1490, the Lyttons built Knebworth, a magnificent mansion which has been substantially altered as the family's circumstances have changed. In its original form Knebworth was a great Tudor courtyard house, augmented in later, Jacobean times with a superb banqueting hall, complete with screen and panelling, and a grand staircase.

The year 1811 saw the start of a massive building programme which transformed both the interior and the exterior of the house. The change was instigated by the Victorian novelist, poet and playwright Edward Bulwer-Lytton, who favoured the ornamental splendours of the high Gothic style.

In the early years of the 20th century Edwin Lutyens and Gertrude Jekyll redesigned the gardens to provide a foil for the neo-Gothic crenellated magnificence of the main building. Today Knebworth is as much a reflection of a 19th-century country house as of an Elizabethan mansion.

LEFT *Knebworth is adorned with heraldic beasts holding shields bearing the armorial crests of the Lyttons, who have lived here more than 500 years*

BELOW *Knebworth's battlements and turrets rise above the surrounding grounds. The country house's most famous resident was Edward Bulwer-Lytton, Victorian author and statesman*

The South Downs

Now a National Park, the South Downs are a long ridge of chalk upland, with an escarpment to the north and a gentle sloping plateau to the south. They stretch across the counties of Sussex and Hampshire, extending from the dizzying heights of Beachy Head to the eastern fringes of Winchester. Small villages of flint, brick and timber hung with pantiles cluster at their foot on either side, but the high ground is empty of settlements – perfect walking, mountain-biking and riding country.

The South Downs Way – a route for walkers, cyclists and riders – follows the old routes and droveways of ancient people along the entire crest of the Downs, passing prehistoric hillforts and tumuli that bear witness to the earliest downland settlers.

Lewes

In a gap in the eastern Downs lies the town of Lewes, a Saxon foundation that retains its medieval street plan, along with many fine old houses, some hung with sham 18th-century bricks known as mathematical tiles. On 5th November each year, bonfire societies from Lewes and other Sussex towns process through the town with flaming torches before lighting huge fires on which are burned effigies of Guy Fawkes and the Pope. This traditionally commemorated the execution of 17 local Protestant martyrs between 1555 and 1557. Today, the celebrations are mainly about local pride and independence and are enjoyed by all members of the community.

LEFT *The view from Fulking Escarpment in the South Downs looks across the hedge-lined fields and woodlands of the Weald, and towards the distant North Downs*

ABOVE *Lewes Castle was founded by the Normans soon after they invaded, although the imposing Barbican, built for show rather than defence, was added later*

ABOVE *HMS* Victory, *the only great wooden battleship to be completely preserved, was built in 1765 and withdrawn from frontline duty seven years after the Battle of Trafalgar*

RIGHT *Taller than the London Eye, the Spinnaker Tower was designed to evoke a ship's mast and gives views along the coast and over the Isle of Wight*

FAR RIGHT *Life below deck on warships like* Victory *was extremely cramped, sailors and gunners slept in hammocks (stowed during the day) right beside the cannons*

Portsmouth

Britain's proud seafaring past meets its modern, streamlined naval present in the city of Portsmouth, located on broad Portsea Island and overlooking the world's second largest natural harbour. Henry VII established a royal dockyard here in the 15th century, and Portsmouth today combines its role as the country's most important naval base with that of a witness to the nation's seagoing past.

The town has numerous museums, many with maritime themes, the foremost of which is the complex of the historic dockyard at the Royal Naval Base. Here is preserved HMS *Victory*, Admiral Lord Nelson's flagship at the Battle of Trafalgar in 1805.

Nelson was fatally wounded in the battle, and the spot below decks where this great hero died is still proudly pointed out by naval guides. Other historic ships on the site include the recovered remains of the Tudor *Mary Rose*, Henry VIII's flagship, which capsized spectacularly in 1545, drowning most of the 700-strong crew before the King's eyes. The youngest vessel here, Britain's very first iron-clad warship HMS *Warrior*, the largest and fastest ship of the day, dates from 1860. The nearby Royal Naval Museum tells the full story of British naval history.

Although badly damaged by bombing in the Second World War, the city has some attractive corners, notably Old Portsmouth (the original town by the harbour entrance), with Georgian buildings along a cobbled street and the much-altered 12th-century cathedral. Above the water's edge, Tudor fortifications look out over the ceaseless comings and goings on the waters of the Solent, which bustle with modern naval vessels, pleasure boats and the regular ferries to France and the Isle of Wight.

There are staggering views from the enclosed viewing platform of the Spinnaker Tower, a high sleek, modern structure standing at 558 feet (170m) on Gunwharf Quay, the waterside stretch of stylish shops, bars and restaurants that represents the 21st-century Portsmouth.

The New Forest

Nowhere else in this region does the rural present meet the past as strongly as in the New Forest, an expanse of 144 square miles (373sq km) of Hampshire heath, grassland, bog and woodland, requisitioned in 1079 as a royal hunting preserve by William I, and now a National Park.

William enacted draconian Forest Laws to preserve the precious deer, but pressure from forest dwellers forced later monarchs to concede rights to gather fuel and keep stock, many of which still exist. The main privileges, held by the Commoners of the Forest for the last 900 years, include the pasturing of ponies, cattle and pigs in the open forest. Today, Commoners' rights are still overseen by the ancient Court of Verderers, whose role was once to enforce the Forest Law that punished severely anyone who interfered with the deer and their food sources.

Together, Commoners and Crown have shaped the landscape of the forest, whose flora is defined by what the deer and domestic stock will, or will not, eat. The result is a beautiful area of woodland and open country, visited by more than 13 million people annually.

The best way to enjoy it is to walk or ride a horse or mountain bike along the dense network of paths and tracks that weave through the area, before exploring its two loveliest villages, Beaulieu and Bucklers Hard. The latter is an Elizabethan shipyard settlement, where men o' war were once constructed from the giant oaks of the Forest.

Windsor Castle

England's premier castle (and the Queen's favourite royal residence) dates from 1080, when William I built a stronghold on the one defensible site on the Thames west of London. His motte now forms the base of the Round Tower, built by Henry II, the first of a succession of major works that transformed the castle over the centuries. Chief among these was the construction, from 1475 to 1528 in the Lower Ward, of St George's Chapel – a supreme example of Perpendicular Gothic architecture – and the embellishment of the state rooms in the early 19th century. Today, Windsor is a definitive statement of the wealth and power of the monarchy, a remarkable complex of historic buildings whose interiors showcase the finest in architecture, art and interior decoration.

The castle's exterior appearance dates from the early 19th century, when James Wyatt remodelled the towers and battlements, and the silhouette dominates the surrounding town and extensive surrounding parkland. The interior is packed with treasures, including a superb picture collection with works by Holbein, Rubens, Van Dyck, Gainsborough and Canaletto, exquisite wood carving by Grinling Gibbons, fine porcelain and furniture. In 1992, a major fire damaged parts of the castle, and its brilliant restoration illustrates the range of specialist expertise still thriving in modern Britain.

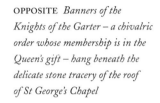

OPPOSITE *Banners of the Knights of the Garter – a chivalric order whose membership is in the Queen's gift – hang beneath the delicate stone tracery of the roof of St George's Chapel*

ABOVE *Windsor Castle is the largest inhabited castle in the world. Despite its battlements and medieval appearance, it is mostly Victorian*

LEFT *When the Queen is in residence at the castle, the Royal Standard is flown from the Round Tower instead of the Union Jack*

Southwest England

Southwest England covers the area south and east of the Bristol Channel: the counties of Wiltshire, Dorset, Somerset, Devon and Cornwall. Far enough west to escape London's magnetic pull, the West Country, as it is also known, is predominantly rural, marked by serene market and cathedral towns, and embraced by some of Britain's most beautiful and geologically diverse coastline.

Bristol, its one major city, lies to the north, with Plymouth to the south. Inland, the centre encompasses rolling countryside and a string of thriving towns, many with history dating back to Roman times. Earlier still, this area was home to prehistoric tribes, whose legacy includes the spectacular monuments of Stonehenge and Avebury on Salisbury Plain. To the west, the ancient Celtic race gave Cornwall its distinctive place names.

The southwest is rich in legend – the home of King Arthur in the 6th century. Some 300 years later the embryonic country of England emerged from Alfred's kingdom of Wessex. Alfred regrouped his forces to fend off the Danes in the heartland of the Somerset Levels, a unique lowland area that was once flooded by the sea.

West from here, the fertile red acres of Devon are interrupted by two great upland areas, Exmoor and Dartmoor. Beyond lies the rugged and beautiful Cornish coastline, with its huddled fishing villages, secluded beaches and windswept ruins of old tin mines that constitutes one of Britain's favourite holiday areas.

The remote fishing village of Clovelly, beneath towering wooded cliffs on the north Devon coast, has a tiny harbour with a slipway and lifeboat station

Stonehenge

Nine miles (14km) north of Salisbury stands the ancient stone structure of Stonehenge, a UNESCO World Heritage Site and one of the most famous and easily recognisable prehistoric monuments in Europe.

Today's monoliths and trilithons – those pairs of upright stones crossed by a lintel – were originally part of a much larger complex, whose significance has been disputed by archaeologists for many years. Theories about Stonehenge's purpose include it being a place of ritual sacrifice and sun worship or an enormous astronomical calendar, as the stones are aligned with the winter and summer solstice.

Construction probably took place in several stages, commencing around 3000BC with the building of the outer banks and ditch and finishing about 1400BC, when the last of the great sandstone trilithons was raised. The stones, known as sarsens, came from the neighbouring Marlborough Downs. The smaller bluestones inside the circle, however, were somehow transported to the site all the way from the Preseli Hills in western Wales. Despite restrictions of access among the actual stones, Stonehenge remains an evocative place, drawing thousands of visitors who come here to celebrate the summer solstice and marvel at Britain's very own ancient wonder of the world.

LEFT *Sunlight illuminates the carefully dressed stone of the trilithons at Stonehenge. It is not known how the inner circle of bluestones were transported from Wales*

The Dorset Coast

Dorset's coastline forms the sea fringe of one of southern England's loveliest and most rural counties; a glorious stretch of beaches, downs and cliffs that runs from Bournemouth in the east to Lyme Regis in the west. The area draws hordes of summer visitors who come to enjoy traditional seaside holidays at resorts like Swanage and Weymouth, walk the South West Coast Path and explore rewarding small towns such as Bridport and Lyme Regis.

Lyme, a classy little town packed with Georgian houses and fronted by the solid stone mass of the curving harbour wall known as the Cobb, has drawn fossil hunters ever since the 18th century. The geologically complex structure of the cliffs here, which are known as the Jurassic Coast, provides perfect conditions for fossil preservation, while their inherent softness causes frequent landslips that expose the fossils. In 1811, Mary Anning, a 12-year-old local girl, discovered an almost complete ichthyosaurus skeleton measuring 33 feet (10m), now found in London's Natural History Museum.

ABOVE *A huge ammonite is revealed on a rock on the beach near Lyme Regis, beneath crumbling cliffs that doubtless contain many more fossils yet to be discovered*

RIGHT *The rolling chalk of Swyre Head and Bat's Head, west of Durdle Door, is stiff walking for the many hikers on the South West Coast Path*

OPPOSITE *With its breathtaking sequences of views and constant changes in level, Dorset's coastline has some of the finest and most challenging clifftop walking in the West Country, such as around Golden Cap*

RIGHT *The perfect curve of Lulworth Cove, east of Weymouth, was formed when the sea broke through the sandstone of the cliffs and eroded the land*

BELOW *Like Lulworth Cove, the limestone natural arch of Durdle Door was formed by sea erosion over thousands of years. Eventually, it will collapse*

East of Lyme rise huge sandstone cliffs, with Golden Cap, at 627 feet (191m) the highest point on the coast, providing a superb vantage point over the whole of Lyme Bay. East again, the cliffs give way to the more gently rolling green hills that back Chesil Beach, an extraordinary wide storm beach of pebbles 50 feet (15m) high and 17 miles (27km) long. Due to the action of wickedly strong coastal currents, the beach's pebbles range from fist-size at Portland in the east to 'pea gravel' at Burton Bradstock in the west.

As you continue east, Weymouth is the main resort on this stretch of the coast, a perfect base for exploring Lulworth, the Isle of Portland and the Purbeck Hills.

The last of these mark the entrance to the Isle of Purbeck – not really an island, but a promontory of heathland south of Poole Harbour, with a distinctively insular feel. It contains the pretty village of Corfe Castle, over which rise the ruins of the castle itself, once a Royalist stronghold, which was besieged and taken by the Roundheads during the English Civil War.

Poole Harbour is a huge expanse of water, which contains wooded Brownsea Island, a haven for red squirrels, sika deer and wading birds. Poole itself adjoins Bournemouth, a resort and favoured retirement town founded in 1811, with a glorious sandy beach and neatly tended stretches of public gardens.

BELOW *Crowning a hill in a breach in the Purbeck ridge, Corfe Castle was dismantled during the Civil War in 1646 and remains a spectacular, jagged ruin*

Bath

The city of Bath lies on either side of the River Avon in a bowl of hills, up whose slopes are stacked Georgian terraces built during the city's 18th-century heyday as England's leading spa, where fashionable society flocked to take the waters for their health.

Centuries earlier, Bath developed as Roman Britain's top spa town, named *Aquae Sulis*, with a magnificent bathing complex that included the Great Bath, 110 feet (33.5m) in length. Today it is fed by the same spring, whose waters remain at a constant 46.5ºC.

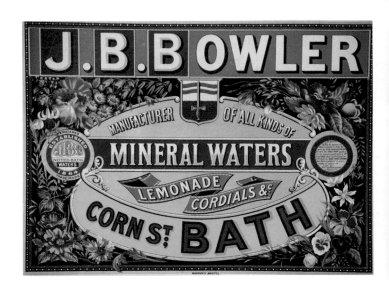

By 1720, Bath was once more in vogue with the leisured classes, and two architects – father and son, both named John Wood – were responsible for the city's transformation from a medieval town with a fine abbey to England's most perfect Georgian ensemble. They designed a whole new town, with classically inspired streets, a Royal Crescent and Circus; at the Assembly Rooms, a hub of 18th-century social life, visitors gathered for gossip and entertainment. Later architects added the Pump Room, Pulteney Bridge and more terraces and squares.

Today, Bath offers some of the best shopping, eating and cultural life in the whole of the southwest, and visitors can now once again luxuriate in Britain's only natural thermal waters at the recently created Thermae Bath Spa.

ABOVE *John Wood designed the Royal Crescent, built between 1767 and 1775, a graceful curve that is considered one of Europe's great architectural set pieces*

RIGHT *Pulteney Bridge, designed by Robert Adam and completed in 1773, spans the River Avon and is lined with tiny shops and flanked by an elegant arcade*

Exmoor

The high plateau of Exmoor rises to the south of the Bristol Channel, a National Park extending across part of north Somerset and into Devon and which is cut through by the wooded river valleys of the Exe, the Barle, and the East and West Lyn, which meet at Lynmouth.

Its long coastline, at 30 miles (48km), is both dramatic and beautiful, with the highest cliffs in England, while inland are lonely moorlands and high, rolling pastures, much of which formed the former royal hunting ground of Exmoor Forest.

Exmoor has a good network of footpaths and bridleways, tracks that traverse what, in bad weather, can be some of England's most forbidding landscapes.

The upland heart is home to wonderfully diverse flora and fauna, including birds of prey, England's only wild population of red deer, and the unique Exmoor ponies. This stocky species, thought to be closely related to prehistoric horses, can be seen grazing the treeless wastes at the centre of the moor around remote Simonsbath, on the River Barle, downstream of which Tarr Steps is an ancient 17-span clapper bridge built of slabs. Snuggled into the valleys are the villages of Exford, not far from the heathery heights of Dunkery Beacon and postcard-pretty Winsford, with its array of thatched cottages.

Exmoor's northern edge runs along the sea to the west of Minehead, the starting point for England's longest and

most spectacular long-distance footpath, the South West Coast Path, which runs for 630 miles (1,014km) around the southwest tip of the country.

In Exmoor, the path passes through Porlock, a village cupped by hills and crammed with thatch-and-cob houses. It was 'a person on business from Porlock' who famously interrupted Samuel Taylor Coleridge as he scribbled down his opium-induced poem 'Kubla Khan', in 1797 – the epic work was never completed.

The best time to explore Exmoor is in summer, when the heathland is painted with spreads of gorse, ling and bell heather, and the views down to the coastal resorts of Lynton and Lynmouth are particularly inspirational.

ABOVE *Dunkery Beacon, at 1,703 feet (519m), is Exmoor's highest point. It gives superb views north towards the Bristol Channel and as far as the Brecon Beacons in Wales*

BELOW *Exmoor's coast is unusual in that moorland extends to the cliff tops, as seen here at remote Woody Bay and Lee Bay, west of Lynton*

Resorts of the Southwest

ABOVE *Punch and Judy shows probably originated during the restoration of Charles II in the 17th century and are still part of the seaside holiday experience*

The West Country is seaside holiday country par excellence, with resorts that fit the bill for every variety of pleasure seeker.

Mass air travel to the Mediterranean lured thousands away from England in the 1970s, forcing many traditional centres to sharpen up their acts and provide alternative diversions for those inevitable English summer days when the sun does not shine. Weymouth is a case in point – an old port that was transformed into a booming Victorian resort, complete with Esplanade and golden sand, and which now pulls in the 21st-century trippers with its sea-oriented visitor attractions. Further west, Torquay and the surrounding Torbay area sells itself as the 'English Riviera', complete with a mini-corniche, exuberant municipal planting and rows of palms, which flourish in this sheltered and sunny spot.

There's nothing sheltered about the wild north coast in the neighbouring county of Cornwall, where the pounding seas hit England's westernmost point at Land's End. The full force of the Atlantic lies behind the waves on this coast, drawing in surfers from all over the world. Their mecca is Newquay, an unashamedly brash, youth-oriented surfers' paradise centred around 7 miles (11km) of wide, sandy beaches, where the breakers rival anything available in the rest of Europe.

The resorts of Cornwall's south coast have a very different appeal. Here, flooded river valleys known as rias penetrate deep inland. They provide marvellously sheltered waters for sailing enthusiasts, who flock to the waters around Fowey, St Mawes, Falmouth (where you'll also find the Cornish branch of the National Maritime Museum) and the wide, wooded Helford River.

RIGHT *Beach huts, like these at Torquay, are a quintessential part of the English beach scene, and are used for changing, sheltering and relaxing*

BELOW *Weymouth's fortunes were enhanced in 1789, when George III came there to recuperate, since when the town has expanded to become one of Dorset's main seaside resorts*

Gardens of the Southwest

Gardening on a grand scale started in the 18th century, when new money paid for big houses and their surrounding grounds, often scattered with classical follies and eye-catchers. Landowners not only employed designers to lay out their parks, but were also the driving force behind the first plant-hunting expeditions that, over the next 200 years, were to see thousands of exotic species taking their place in English gardens.

Stourhead, Wiltshire, is among the finest of these gardens, a magical landscape centred round an artificial lake, created by damming the River Stour. The garden was laid out in 1741 for Henry Hoare, who had returned from a European Grand Tour, his head spinning with visions of a well-ordered natural paradise, dotted with temples, grottoes, bridges and statues.

In contrast to this contrived perfection, Cornish gardens in the 18th and 19th centuries always played a dual role, acting as trial gardens for establishing the rarities collected in China, India and the Himalayas, and providing pleasure parks. South of St Austell, the Lost Gardens of Heligan, rescued from overgrown oblivion in the 1990s by Tim Smit, are still true to this concept, drawing thousands of non-gardening visitors, while acting as a living museum of the grandest type of Victorian garden.

OPPOSITE *The biomes of Cornwall's Eden Project are packed with exotic plants from around the world. Here, the Mediterranean Biome is shown*

ABOVE *Stourhead's very own Pantheon is reflected in the waters of the lake. The planting was conceived to accentuate the buildings on the site*

LEFT *Made from rocks and plants and created by Sue and Pete Hill in 1998, this humorous Giant's Head is an imaginative addition to the garden at Heligan, capturing the spirit of Victorian ornamentation*

Dartmoor

Dartmoor, in Devon, is southern England's largest wilderness area, an expanse of 365 square miles (945sq km) of moorland and bog where granite tors (gnarled rock outcrops of extraordinary shapes) dominate the skyline. The central plateau is high, wild and lonely, its heathery surface pockmarked with treacherous stretches of marsh and morass and prone to wild weather and impenetrable mist – conditions that seem tailor-made for the Baskerville hound featured in Conan Doyle's famous Sherlock Holmes story, set here. Around the outer edges of the barren centre are softer, greener hills, whose verdant river valleys contain some of this National Park's most characteristic and appealing villages.

LEFT *This derelict engine house, known as Wheal Betsy, is the last surviving structure of its kind on Dartmoor, and attests to Dartmoor's once-flourishing tin-mining industry that existed from before Roman times until 1930*

OPPOSITE ABOVE *Herds of cross-bred Dartmoor ponies graze all over the moor. Each autumn they are rounded up and marked for ownership; some are sold on*

Princetown lies at the heart of the Moor – a dour, granite-built settlement famed for its high-security prison, which was built to house prisoners of the Napoleonic Wars. The village gives access to some of Dartmoor's most beautiful country in the shape of high moors and wooded valleys, and lies within easy reach of two of the prettiest upland villages, Widecombe in the Moor and Buckland. Widecombe, whose venerable church dominates the village centre, will be forever associated with the folk ballad of Uncle Tom Cobley and his band of friends on their journey to Widecombe Fair – an event still held in early September. Dartmeet, where the waters of the East and West Dart converge, lies west of the two villages, a famous beauty spot, which draws thousands of tourists.

To escape the crowds, head north towards Okehampton, where there is superb walking outside prohibited times on the high ground controlled by the Ministry of Defence, which uses this area as a firing range. It's here that the full grandeur of this remote countryside can be experienced, and there are beautiful walking routes up to southern England's two highest points, Yes Tor at 2,028ft (618m) and High Willhays at 2,039 feet (621m).

There's plenty to interest nature lovers on the tops, from the sheer beauty of the wild flowers, which include rare bog plants and wild orchids, to the great variety of birdlife, which ranges from wheeling raptors such as buzzards and kestrels to the cheery stonechats and wagtails to be seen busy in the tumbling streams.

OPPOSITE BELOW *Farmers and tin miners used what are known as clapper bridges to negotiate Dartmoor's main rivers. This one dates from the 13th century and crosses the River Dart at Postbridge*

OVERLEAF *From the granite tors on Dartmoor's high tops, there are superb views over the starkly unpopulated moorland, England's highest and wildest terrain south of the Pennines*

Clovelly

ABOVE *Clovelly's traffic-free cobbled street, sloping steeply to the fishing harbour, is known variously as Up-a-long or Down-a-long according to which direction one is going*

Long before the first tourists discovered the West Country, Devon and Cornwall relied on fishing, farming and mining. Cornish tin mines have long been closed, but farming still flourishes, and fishing communities still cling to the edge of the beautiful and rugged coastline.

On the north Devon coast, the picturesque village of Clovelly lost its fishing industry when the herring stocks disappeared, and today relies solely on tourism. Still privately owned, the village – all painstakingly renovated cobbled streets and flower-hung, slate-roofed cottages – tumbles down a 400 feet (122m) cliff to the tiny harbour, one of the few safe havens on this rocky coast. So steep are its streets that all goods are transported on sledges which, in the 1990s, replaced traditional donkey transport.

Brixham

On the other side of the county, Brixham has been an important fishing port since before William III landed here in 1688 to claim the throne of England, and still supplies fish for the London markets. It's a beguiling place, its harbour packed with fishing boats – diesel-powered today, though a few examples still exist of the beautiful Brixham trawlers, with their distinctive red sails, that were built here until the 1920s. Brixham's fishermen were courageous mariners, sailing as far as the Newfoundland banks as early as the 16th century in search of cod for the European market. Today, the industry goes hand in hand with the town's role as a popular summer resort, whose pleasures centre around its beaches, clifftop walks and highly rated seafood restaurants.

LEFT *A replica of Sir Francis Drake's ship,* the Golden Hind, *in which he circumnavigated the world, shares harbour space at Brixham with the fishing trawlers*

ABOVE *Brixham's stalls are the ideal place to sample fresh shellfish and seafood. One of the most renowned local delicacies is Brixham crab*

St Ives

Fishing boats still sail out from the sheltered harbour of St Ives, far to the west on Cornwall's northern coast, but the great days of the pilchard-fishing industry are over and the town today is better known for its compact charm and artistic connections. It is wonderfully picturesque, with white-sand beaches, narrow, cobbled streets and a jumble of lichen-clad roofs drawing thousands of summertime visitors, who come to enjoy some of the loveliest town beaches in England.

The town, with its extraordinarily pellucid light, attracted waves of artists from the early years of the last century. Among them, in the 1940s, were Ben Nicholson and his second wife, the non-figurative sculptor Barbara Hepworth, who lived in the town from 1949 until her death in 1975. Her studio and remarkable sculpture-filled garden are now a museum, while other examples of her work are scattered around the town, including a gentle Madonna in the 15th-century church of St Ia.

There's more 20th-century art on display at Tate Gallery St Ives, an airy and innovative modern structure overlooking beautiful Porthmeor Beach. Drenched in sea light, the Tate displays sculpture, paintings and ceramics, among which are fine examples of the potter Bernard Leach's Japanese-inspired works, and paintings by the naïve artist and fisherman, Alfred Wallis (1855–1942).

The presence of the gallery has boosted the town's image and St Ives today, with its upmarket restaurants and commercial art galleries, is markedly more sophisticated than when Virginia Woolf described it as 'a windy, noisy, fishy, vociferous, narrow-streeted town' – although she would still recognise the constricted streets and their slate-hung cottages.

ABOVE *Barbara Hepworth found the ideal work place at Trewyn Studio, and designed her garden with the placing of her sculptures amid the greenery uppermost in her mind*

RIGHT *Designed by Evans and Shalev on the site of an old gasworks, Tate Gallery St Ives opened in 1993 to display St Ives School art against the background that inspired it*

OPPOSITE *The idyllic beaches at St Ives attract bathers, surfers, and families enjoying the sands and the dozens of rockpools exposed by the outgoing tides*

Wales

Wales is a country set apart, a distinct cultural and geographic entity that has retained its sense of nationhood for hundreds of years, producing a tangibly different mood that's obvious to anyone passing through the Marches – that deeply rural country along the border with England. Although part of the British Union since 1536, the Welsh people have always kept a firm grip on their language and traditions, making Wales as distinct in its spirit as it is in its rugged mountains, rushing rivers and sinuous coastline.

About a fifth of a population of 2.9 million are fluent Welsh speakers, most of whom live in the north, but the culture associated with the language – the music, the poetry, the love of sport – flourishes as much in the industrial towns and cities of the south as in the rural heartland.

This heartland contains three major hill systems – the Brecon Beacons, the Cambrian Mountains and Snowdonia – and is surrounded on three sides by a coastline of great beauty. In much of rural Wales, hill farming has long been the traditional way of life, and sheep are very much part of the landscape.

Wales' major cities, Cardiff and Swansea, once dependent on shipping, coal mining and steel, have reinvented themselves as buzzing 21st-century centres, their once derelict docklands redeveloped for leisure. More than half the population live in the major towns, but all share the same pride in the country, and understand that nostalgic melancholy known as *hiraeth*, an emotion as quintessentially Welsh as the tradition of *croeso* (welcome) that greets all visitors.

Seen from the top of Snowdon, high ridges create the Snowdon Horseshoe, one of Britain's finest mountain walking routes, which takes in the summit of Crib Goch, towering above a series of lakes

Cardiff

ABOVE *A statue of a coal miner stands on the docks in Cardiff, commemorating those who brought prosperity to the region*

ABOVE *Daubed with the colours of the Welsh flag, rugby fans demonstrate the Welsh passion for their national flag and their love of song*

BELOW *The opening of Cardiff's Millennium Centre for the arts in 2004 reinforced Welsh national pride. The architect Percy Thomas responded to the brief that the building should be 'unmistakably Welsh and internationally outstanding'*

Cardiff's major development and wealth grew from the 18th-century Industrial Revolution, when the Bute family opened up the coal fields of the Welsh valleys and built Cardiff Docks. They transformed the city into one of the world's busiest ports, attracting an ethnically diverse population, many of whom lived in the Tiger Bay district. Industry declined after the Second World War, but the city received a boost in 1955 when Cardiff was proclaimed capital of Wales. The centre was rebuilt around fine Victorian buildings such as City Hall and the Law Courts, while the university and the establishment of the Welsh Assembly in 1998, put the city firmly on the international scene. Cardiff Bay has been transformed into a superb leisure and recreational complex, and the Millennium Stadium, opened in 1999, is acknowledged as one of Britain's most exciting engineering projects.

Swansea and the Gower

Swansea, Wales' second largest city, proudly displays its industrial heritage in its redeveloped Maritime Quarter, where 19th-century buildings house museums and the Dylan Thomas Centre, Wales' national literature centre. Music, in the form of a major annual festival, plays a large part in the city's cultural life.

Swansea is the gateway to the scenic microcosm that is the Gower peninsula. The pastoral interior of this promontory, some 15 miles (24km) long, is scattered with castles and unspoiled villages, while its coastline ranges from the jagged limestone cliffs of the south to the sand and mud flats around Burry Inlet to the north. Its westernmost point is the Worm's Head, an impressive headland that takes its name from the Old English *orme*, meaning 'dragon'. From here, sweeping beaches, only accessible on foot, stretch north from Rhossili.

ABOVE *A solitary house overlooks the huge sweep of open sands by Rhossili Bay, at the western end of the Gower. The Downs, rising behind, are popular with paragliders*

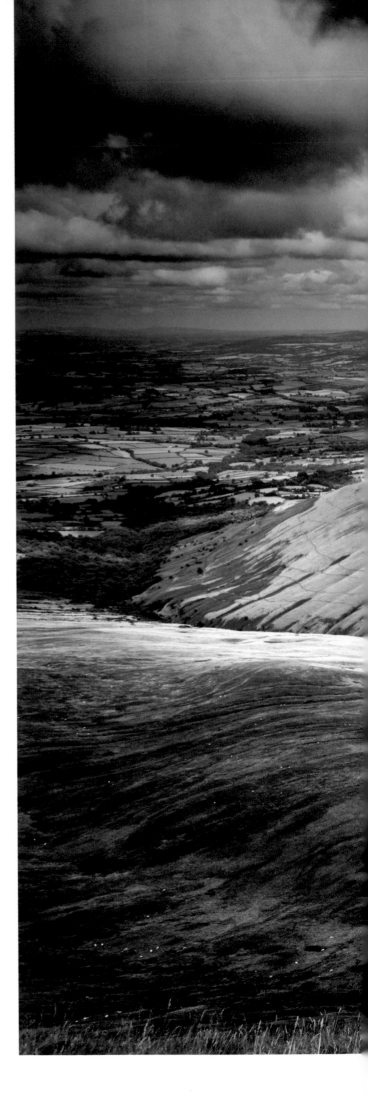

The Brecon Beacons

ABOVE *Sgwd Gwladys in Glynneath is one of a series of waterfalls that tumble in precipitous wooded valleys in the south of the National Park*

RIGHT *Formed of strikingly red sandstone, the high points of the Brecon Beacons comprise a series of precipitously edged ridges that make for some of the finest walking in south Wales*

North of the densely populated towns of south Wales lie the Brecon Beacons, a spread of hills and valleys that was designated a National Park in 1957. This beautiful area of farming country, rich in history, is scattered with small towns and villages where Welsh cultural traditions are preserved. Above it all rise the windswept mountains and open moorland.

The park covers an area of 519 square miles (1,344sq km) and stretches from Carmarthenshire in the west through Monmouthshire, and is bounded by the English border. Its hills form a quartet of upland ranges, whose central massif is the Brecon Beacons proper, high country containing Pen y Fan, at 2,907 feet (886m) the highest peak in south Wales, and the Beacons Horseshoe, a magnificent ridge which draws thousands of walkers from the neighbouring coastal urban areas. East of here are the Black Mountains stretching from Abergavenny in the Usk valley to Crickhowell and north to Hay-on-Wye, from

which a spectacular mountain road heads over the Gospel Pass and past the majestic ruins of Llanthony Priory. To the west of the central spurs are Fforest Fawr, the dramatic waterfalls of the Hepste, Nedd Fechan and Mellte gorges, and the high tops of the Black Mountain, a remote area good for high-level walking along the Carmarthen Fans. Besides catering for serious walkers, the park attracts thousands who enjoy the fresh air, views and wildlife. Llangorse Lake (Llyn Syfaddan), the largest natural lake in south Wales, is a favourite with sailors and windsurfers.

Local towns combine a role as service centres for the surrounding hamlets and remote farms, providing accommodation and activities for visitors, and some have built a reputation on very specialised attractions. Brecon itself is one of these, an ancient riverside settlement named for a Welsh chieftan, Brychan. Today it's an appealing town, with a serene and austere parish church that became a cathedral in 1923, and home to a renowned Jazz Festival every August. It's also the start of the partially restored Monmouthshire and Brecon Canal, which slices southwards through the National Park and ends at Cwmbran.

East of here, near the English border, Hay-on-Wye is a bibliophile's heaven. This is a tiny town, well known for its second-hand bookshops, and virtually every building, including the castle and former cinema, is dedicated to bookselling in one way or another. Hay's famous early-summer Festival of Literature, established in 1988, pulls in all the best-known names in the publishing world.

BELOW *Pen y Fan can be seen in clear conditions from points as distant as Shropshire and Devon. Llangorse Lake, in the foreground, has yielded evidence of an Iron Age settlement on a man-made island*

To the south, and easily reached from Cardiff and Newport, the pretty town of Crickhowell is packed with restaurants and gastropubs. It bills itself as 'the Gourmet Capital of South Wales', with restaurant menus making the most of superb local produce. North from here is Tretower Court, a stately example of an early Welsh 'gentleman's residence', complete with a 12th-century military keep and a magnificent Great Hall. The house is surrounded by a re-creation of the original 15th-century garden.

South of Crickhowell, the National Park ends and gives way to the valleys of south Wales, once busy with coal mining and iron production. Merthyr Tydfil and the World Heritage Site of Blaenavon are part of this fascinating industrial legacy.

RIGHT ABOVE *In the Brecon Beacons Waterfall Country, the rivers Hepste, Mellte and Nedd Fechan have cut through layers of sandstone and shale to create a series of dramatic gorges and waterfalls*

RIGHT BELOW *The Monmouthshire and Brecon Canal runs 35 miles (56km) from here in Brecon and along the Usk valley, with a towpath along its length. It is popular for boating and canoeing*

The Pembrokeshire Coast

One of Britain's great walks skirts the whole of the Pembrokeshire Coast in the shape of a long path that runs for 180 miles (290km) from Amroth in the south to St Dogmaels in the north. It's demanding but spectacular walking, which includes 35,000 feet (10,670m) of ascent and descent over its course, and takes in the most scenic section of the Welsh coast, with craggy headlands, towering cliffs, dunes and sweeping beaches.

Since 1970, this part of Wales has been a National Park, whose confines stretch some miles inland and also include the offshore islands of Skomer, Skokholm, Ramsey, Grassholm and Caldey, all rich in seabirds and holding large seal colonies. To the south lie the broad sheltered waters of Milford Haven, while north rise the Preseli Hills,

windswept moorland from where prehistoric humans quarried the bluestones used for the construction of Stonehenge in Wiltshire.

Of the low-key settlements that hug the coast, St David's, with its cathedral dedicated to Wales' patron saint, is the most beguiling. This ancient Celtic settlement lies around Glyn Rhosyn (the Vale of the Rose), a sheltered, rising bowl containing the cathedral, which dates from the 1180s. Flooded with light, the interior has been expanded and altered over the centuries but retains a deep sense of spirituality, in marked contrast to the grandeur of the ruined Bishop's Palace, built in the 13th century and expanded to include a magnificent Great Hall by Bishop Henry de Gower in 1328.

BELOW *On the site of St David's 6th-century monastery, the cathedral of St David is built on a slope, so visitors literally walk 'up' the aisle*

RIGHT *Thousands of puffins visit the offshore islands from March to August to breed in colonies and return to the same burrows each year*

BELOW *From its craggy summit, Carn Llidi, above St David's Head looks out towards the island of Ramsey, an RSPB reserve with large breeding colonies of kittiwakes and other seabirds*

Portmeirion and Porthmadog

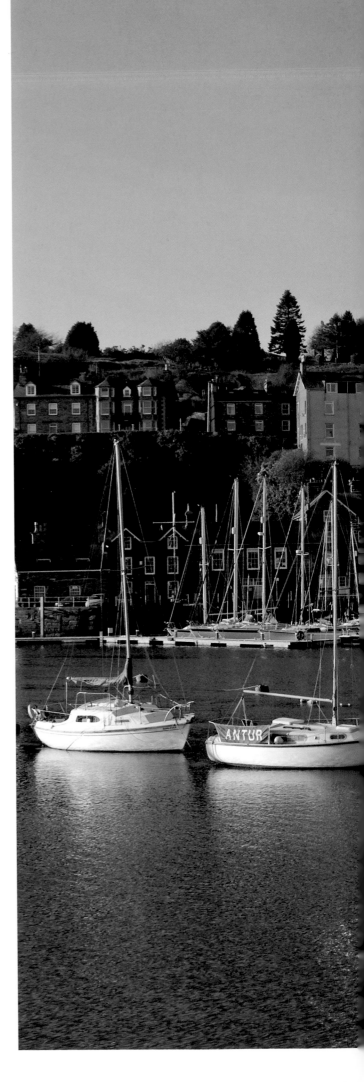

ABOVE *Portmeirion's extraordinary buildings reflect a wide range of European architectural styles. Through this, Clough Williams-Ellis aimed to show that such development could enhance a beautiful and natural landscape*

RIGHT *Porthmadog grew rich on slate, which was brought by rail from quarries at Blaenau Ffestiniog and then shipped from this harbour, with its many slate-roofed houses*

Set on wooded slopes above the sheltered waters of Traeth Bach, south of Snowdon, lies the extraordinary Italianate village of Portmeirion. It was the brainchild of Clough Williams-Ellis, whose life-long preoccupations were architecture, landscape design and conservation. He purchased the site in 1925, and by 1939 the most distinctive buildings had been erected, though he worked on the details until 1975. Classical façades, cupolas, onion domes and steeples embellish the buildings, many of which were rescued from demolition in other parts of Britain, and this magical fantasy is surrounded by sub-tropical gardens and miles of sandy beaches.

North from here is the harbour town of Porthmadog, named for its founder W A Maddocks, an 18th-century entrepreneur who built a great embankment, the Cob, across the Glaslyn estuary. This formed a natural harbour from which thousands of tons of slate from the mines at Blaenau Ffestiniog were shipped all over the world.

Snowdonia

North Wales is the stronghold of the Welsh language and all that signifies, and contains Snowdonia. Here, in the highest land in England and Wales, at 3,560 feet (1,085m), Snowdon is the highest mountain, dominating a swathe of dramatic upland country. Since 1951, the area has been a National Park, drawing millions of visitors, but it's also home to more than 25,000 people who live and work in its towns and villages or make their living on the hill farms.

The English gave Snowdonia its familiar name. Welsh speakers still call the region Eryri, the 'abode of the eagles', and for them it is the historic heartland of the country, forever associated with the heroes Llywelyn ap Gruffydd (d.1282) and Owain Glyndwr (c.1354–1416)

Snowdonia was one of the first of Britain's wild regions to enter the public consciousness when late 18th-century travellers, no longer able to visit Europe, because of the

disruption of the Napoleonic Wars, came here and found rugged landscape that rivalled anything across the Channel. Much of the area's wealth came from the great slate deposits in the hills, mined extensively in the 19th century to roof houses as far away as Australia. The slate industry was centred on the small town of Blaenau Ffestiniog, where the Llechwedd Slate Caverns are part of a working mine and open to visitors.

From here, the road heads north to Betws-y-Coed, a settlement located beautifully in gentler, wooded countryside and renowned for waterfalls that can be found in the surrounding hills. To the southwest, the coastline draws as many visitors as the hills, with thousands enjoying the vast beaches round Cardigan Bay every year. Barmouth, just north of the Mawddach estuary, is the main resort along the western coast.

OPPOSITE *Near Harlech, this paved trod known as the Roman Steps gives access to the Rhinogs, which constitute some of the wildest and otherwise most impenetrable terrain in Snowdonia*

BELOW *Snowdonia's climate often sees severe conditions during winter, when snow transforms the landscape of the high mountains into a majestic alpine scene*

Great Little Railways of North Wales

In clear weather the view from the summit of Snowdon is one of the most memorable in Wales. For those who prefer not to tackle the walk up, the Snowdon Mountain Railway provides a memorable alternative ascent. Britain's only rack railway, it runs from the old slate town of Llanberis up the rocky mountain slopes to the very top of the mountain. Feisty little trains are very much part of the Welsh experience, with numerous small independent lines, affectionately known as the Great Little Railways, and the narrow-gauge Ffestiniog Railway, running the 13 miles (21km) from Porthmadog on the coast to Blaenau Ffestiniog, takes first prize. Built in the 1830s to transport slate from the quarries to the coast for shipment, its wagons were originally horse-drawn, converting to steam and carrying the first passengers in the 1860s. Ten years later, the bogie coach was invented for the railway, and two of these carriages are still in service.

Elsewhere in Snowdonia, further narrow-gauge lines, complete with steam locomotives, polished brass and shiny paintwork, run through some of the park's most splendid scenery. North of Snowdon, the Llanberis Lake Railway runs along the shores of Llyn Padarn, almost connecting with the mountain line. At Bala, on the eastern edge of the National Park, a wonderfully scenic line, dating from 1868, runs along the shore of Wales' largest natural lake, Llyn Tegid (Bala Lake). Llangollen, to the east, has its own railway, which chugs up the Dee valley to Carrog.

BELOW *The brightly painted carriages of the Snowdon Mountain Railway are dwarfed by the hills above the Llanberis Pass as the train approaches Snowdon's summit*

Further south, the Vale of Rheidol line was the last steam railway owned by British Rail. The company operated the narrow-gauge track, that now runs 12 miles (18km) inland from Aberystwyth, until 1989. It was built in 1902 to transport lead down to the coast, and the line is among the most rugged in Britain, with spectacular views throughout and walks through the wooded gauge to the thundering Mynach Falls at Devil's Bridge.

BELOW AND LEFT *Wales's heritage railways include all manner of old engines and carriages. The Llangollen Railway, seen here at Berwyn station, has a variety of rolling stock that once ran on Britain's national rail network*

Anglesey

To the Welsh people, Ynys Môn, the island of Anglesey, is redolent with history and culture – a treasure house of prehistoric sites and the legendary home of the Druid priesthood. It lies across the Menai Straits off the northwest coast of Wales, linked to the mainland by two bridges: a graceful suspension bridge, designed by Thomas Telford in 1826, which soars 100 feet (30.5m) above the water, and Robert Stephenson's sturdier tubular span of 1850, partly rebuilt in 1971. From here, Telford's toll road (now the A5) arrows straight across the island to the port of Holyhead, Anglesey's largest town and the main departure point for ferries to Ireland.

Smaller by far is the village famed for having the longest place name in Britain: Llanfairpwllgwyngyllgogery-chwyrndrobwllllantysiliogogogoch, commonly abbreviated to Llanfair PG. Top of the island's most popular sites is the great castle at Beaumaris, built by Edward I to guard the Menai Straits. Plas Newydd, a magnificently sited 18th-century mansion, is known for its huge canvas by Rex Whistler (1905–44), full of trompe l'oeil effects.

LEFT *Crowned by a lighthouse, South Stack, at the far western point of Anglesey, is a dramatic headland which attracts great numbers of seabirds*

BELOW *Beaumaris, though never completed, is architecturally the most perfect of British medieval castles. Its fortifications were protected by a moat and a tidal dock, allowing ships to sail right up to the walls*

Conwy

One of the finest of Edward I's chain of castles built to subdue the unruly Welsh, Conwy Castle is a blatant and potent symbol of royal power, built between 1283 and 1289. Its soaring curtain walls and eight massive towers rise from a rocky outcrop above the Conwy estuary and enclose a classic two-warded interior, and a Great Hall 125 feet (38m) long.

The drums of the towers are echoed in the design of this town's two historic bridges: Thomas Telford's graceful suspension bridge of 1825, and Robert Stephenson's 1848 railway bridge, the world's first tubular bridge, comprising an iron box tube through which trains run.

Encircled by medieval walls, Conwy also has a notable example of medieval domestic architecture. Aberconwy House (National Trust) was built around 1490 as a merchant's dwelling, and its timbered upper storeys contrast with the stonework of the ground floor.

Llandudno

Just 4 miles (6.4km) north of Conwy, and distinctly less warlike, lies the coastal resort of Llandudno, with its ample seafront crescent and two beaches. The town was developed from a fishing village in the 19th century by Owen Williams, and is built on a grid plan of wide, tree-lined streets. From its spacious late-Victorian houses visitors could stroll (and still do) along the colourfully planted promenade to the elegant pier, 2,295 feet (700m) in length and constructed in 1878.

From the town, Marine Drive circles the perimeter of the Great Orme, a headland to the west, up which runs a cable-hauled tram. The Great Orme is riddled with ancient mine workings – 4,000 years ago copper from deep below the surface was traded all across Europe. A statue of the White Rabbit on the beach here celebrates Llandudno's links with *Alice's Adventures in Wonderland* author, Lewis Carroll (1832–98); it is said that he wrote part of the famous story while in the town.

BELOW *An elegant crescent of Victorian stucco-fronted buildings curves around the bay at Llandudno, a thoroughly traditional resort spectacularly set beneath hills*

The Vale of Llangollen

Shadowed by the Ruabon Mountains, the River Dee runs through the beautiful green Vale of Llangollen in north Wales. The valley takes its name from St Collen, a 7th-century saint who rode through here looking for a place to found his hermitage. The valley was already a holy place – Castell Dinas, above the town, was claimed as the burial site of King Arthur's Holy Grail, and the castle's 13th-century owner, Madog ap Gruffydd Maelor, was to establish the nearby Cistercian monastery of Valle Crucis.

By 1345, Llangollen gained a solid stone bridge, which proved a vital link during the early 19th century when Thomas Telford improved the road through here as part of the main coaching route from London to Holyhead. Telford was also responsible for the soaring 19 arches of the Pontcysyllte Aqueduct, at a height of 127 feet (39m), Britain's largest, which carries the Llangollen Canal across the valley in an iron trough 1,000 feet (305m) long.

ABOVE *Narrowboats squeeze their way the trough that carries the Llangollen Canal across the Pontcysyllte Aqueduct, opened in 1805. The canal has carried tourists as well as goods since the day it was built*

ABOVE *Viewed from the River Dee, the Pontcysyllte Aqueduct majestically adorns the natural landscape. This, and the nearby Horseshoe Falls, engineered by Thomas Telford as a feeder from the river to the canal, form a World Heritage Site*

OPPOSITE *The ruins of 12th-century Castell Dinas overlook the Vale of Llangollen, a natural route west through the hills to Snowdonia and the coast*

Better communications brought a stream of well-known visitors to the Vale, many of whom in the 18th and early 19th centuries stayed with the two 'Ladies of Llangollen' at Plas Newydd, an exuberantly decorated black-and-white picturesque cottage surrounded by Gothic gardens. Visitors still flock to Llangollen, some to fish the Dee for trout and salmon, some to walk in the surrounding hills. The vast majority come in July, when the town hosts the Llangollen International Eisteddfod, a celebration of music, poetry and culture.

Central England

Central England comprises the sweep of land, north of London, that stretches from the Welsh Marches in the west to the lonely Suffolk and Norfolk coasts in the east. The West Midlands were the birthplace of the technological triumphs of the Industrial Revolution in the 18th and 19th centuries; the large industrial central belt includes pottery-manufacturing towns within Stoke-on-Trent and the conurbation around Birmingham, Britain's second largest city.

This is England's geographical heart, densely populated but retaining rural areas of striking beauty and contrast. The hillier areas lie to the west, with the rolling hills of the Cotswolds and the slender ridge of the Malverns either side of the fruit-growing Vale of Evesham, and the chalk hills of the Chilterns further south. To the east are the watery flatlands of East Anglia, and towns and villages whose architecture represents the full flowering of every English style. England's two oldest university cities, Oxford and Cambridge, lie within the region, while its greatest writer, William Shakespeare, was born at Stratford-upon-Avon.

Central England's historical wealth was mainly founded on wool, and merchant money built the country houses and stately manors found throughout the region. Wool money, too, paid for glorious cathedrals such as Norwich, and dozens of fine churches.

In Birmingham's revitalised Bull Ring,
this branch of Selfridges opened in 2003,
and is clad in 15,000 aluminium discs,
continuing the company's tradition for
architectural innovation

RIGHT *Cut by steep-sided valleys, the Long Mynd lies entirely in Shropshire but gives a foretaste of the higher land found a little further west in Wales*

BELOW *Black-and-white half-timbered cottages are a keynote of Marches architecture. The Feathers Hotel in Ludlow has a particularly striking exterior*

Ludlow and the Marches

Founded in 1085, when the first castle was constructed, Ludlow is a Marches town – one of a string of fortified border settlements built to keep out the Welsh. The castle was extended in the 12th and 13th centuries. By 1473, it was the seat of government for the lawless Marches and important enough to act as a royal prison, housing the boy Prince of Wales and his brother before their mysterious deaths in the Tower of London.

Ludlow town, sited on a hill above the Teme and Corve rivers, grew up around the castle, an enclosed and protected settlement surrounded by walls, well-preserved stretches of which still exist. Within this area, the original medieval street layout is lined with over five hundred listed historic buildings, many of them half-timbered

or of Georgian brick. Most famous of these is the Feathers Hotel, a splendid black-and-white carved and timbered Jacobean building, which has been open for business since 1619. The town today is renowned for its exceptional restaurants, its superb seasonal food markets and its drama, music and food festivals.

This area is famed for its association with A E Housman, who idealised its rural charms in his collection of lyrical poems, *A Shropshire Lad* (1896). Housman is buried in St Lawrence's Church, Ludlow. His romantic view of this area is perfectly embodied by Stokesay Castle, northwest of the town, purchased by Laurence de Ludlow in the late 13th century. Ludlow added a great hall, tower and solar to the original 11th-century building, creating a

picture-perfect manor house that bridges the gap between fortified and domestic architecture.

Some 20 miles (32km) northwest of Ludlow, the heath-covered ridge of the Long Mynd straddles the border. This is great walking country, and the Mynd is criss-crossed by footpaths, many of them offering sweeping views to the Black Mountains in Wales. The hikers' base of Church Stretton is a picturesque village complete with the ancient church of St Laurence, parts of which date from Norman times. From here a favourite walk leads up Carding Mill Valley, a gentle and beautiful vale, with paths leading to the top of the Long Mynd ridge.

BELOW *An Iron Age hillfort at the summit of Caer Caradoc surveys a wide sweep of the Welsh Marches. The town of Church Stretton was nicknamed 'Little Switzerland' because of its position among the hills*

The Cotswolds

Spreading a hundred miles through Oxfordshire, Gloucestershire, Wiltshire and touching other counties too, the limestone Cotswolds are uplands, or 'wolds', originally full of 'cots', or sheep enclosures. England's medieval wool trade brought wealth to the area, and it was the merchants and sheep farmers who first used the glorious honey-coloured local stone to build their towns, villages, churches and manor houses. This widespread use of a homogenous building material is the key to the region's appeal, a charm that lures visitors to its timeless settlements, windy ridges and gentle valleys.

There are few large towns in the Cotswolds. Cirencester, an important Roman centre, is the 'capital', a delightful melange of handsome buildings centred around the Market Place and dominated by the 15th-century parish church of St John the Baptist.

Other Cotswold centres include Chipping Campden, a perfectly preserved medieval wool town complete with a fine church, market hall and almshouses; bustling Chipping Norton; Burford, whose glorious High Street slopes down to a bridge over the River Windrush; and Moreton-in-Marsh, a buzzing market town.

But generally, it's the villages that steal the show, a string of idyllic small settlements largely untouched by the modern development and crowds of the towns. They have names such as Bibury, Broadway, Bourton-on-the-Water, Upper and Lower Slaughter, Swinbrook, Great Tew and Northleach, and all feature mullion-windowed cottages with undulating roofs, prosperous farms and splendid churches, a dream of England that inspired the 19th-century Arts and Crafts Movement. This was led by William Morris from his base at Kelmscott Manor, a house dating back to the 16th century and decorated and furnished with Morris's own designs and those of his talented friends, Edward Burne-Jones and William de Morgan.

Tucked in the valleys are numerous great manor houses such as Chastleton House, Sudeley Castle and Snowshill Manor. The wonderfully eccentric Sezincote is an early 19th-century confection inspired by Indian Moghul architecture, while Blenheim Palace, on the eastern fringes of the Cotswolds, remains a powerful statement of the wealth and position of the Dukes of Marlborough. The Roman villa at Chedworth hints that the moneyed classes have for long enjoyed country life here.

RIGHT *This line of old cottages is in Broadway, a particularly handsome village lying at the foot of the western escarpment*

BELOW *The Cotswold Way, 100 miles (161km) long, is carefully routed to take in the area's scenic highlights. Turf-topped Painswick Beacon stands at the convergence of five valleys, the panorama stretching south towards Stroud*

OVER *Blenheim Palace, the birthplace of Sir Winston Churchill, is an outstanding example of English baroque architecture, and lies in magnificent parkland landscaped in the 1760s by 'Capability' Brown*

LEFT *St Lawrence's Church in Bourton-on-the-Water has a 14th-century chancel but gained a new tower in 1784 and was remodelled in Victorian times, when this porch was added*

RIGHT *Held on the spring bank holiday, the cheese-rolling event at Coopers Hill features competitors rolling and pursuing double Gloucester cheeses – a tradition thought to date back some 200 years*

BELOW *A handsome triple-arched bridge spans the River Coln at an idyllic corner of Bibury, overlooked by the 17th-century Swan Hotel*

INSIDE *The village of Miserden is within an estate owned by the Wills family since 1913 and includes a magnificent garden, open to the public, with topiary designed by Edwin Lutyens*

ABOVE *A post box stands out against the hue of locally quarried building stone, which varies subtly across the Cotswolds*

LEFT *The Market Cross at Castle Combe was erected in the 14th century and sits at the convergence of the village's three main streets*

BELOW *Broadway Tower, located between Evesham and Moreton-in-Marsh, is a folly built in 1799; it is 55 feet (17m) tall*

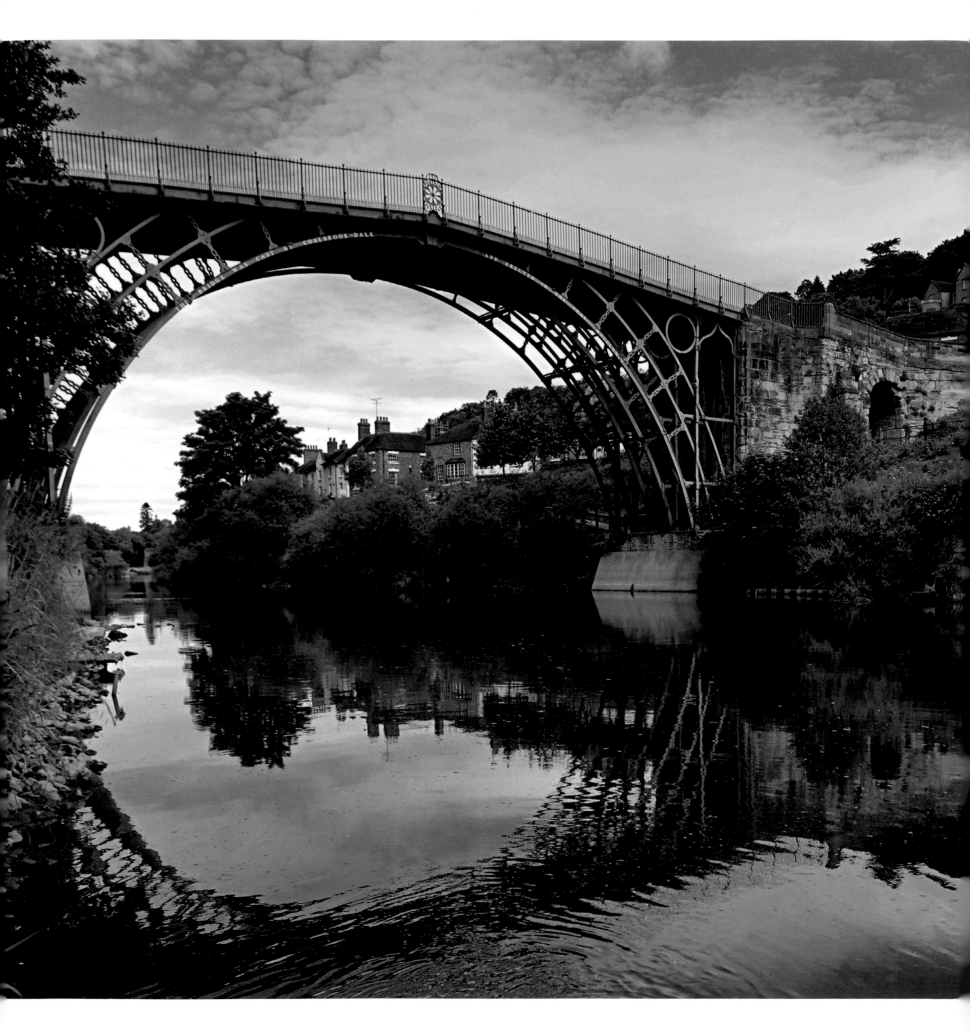

Ironbridge

Southeast of Shropshire's county town of Shrewsbury, the River Severn enters a gorge, the cradle of Britain's Industrial Revolution. It was here, in 1709, that Abraham Darby started iron-smelting using coke rather than charcoal, a development that enabled the invention of a process of making cast iron malleable.

His grandson, another Abraham, reaped the benefits, becoming the engineer responsible for the world's first iron bridge, a graceful single span of 100 feet (30m) that arches

high above the Severn. It was completed in 1779, and its success did much to kick-start the giant strides in industrial manufacture throughout the West Midlands.

Up and down the gorge factories and furnaces were built, employing thousands of people engaged in smelting and the production of heavy-duty iron pieces on a scale unmatched anywhere else in the world.

By the 20th century industry had moved elsewhere and Ironbridge Gorge's importance declined. It was only towards the end of the century that it was recognised as one of the world's most important industrial historic sites and given UNESCO World Heritage status. Today the gorge's buildings house ten fascinating museums devoted to Britain's industrial past. They include Coalbrookdale iron foundry and Blists Hill, with its collection of industrial buildings, many brought from around the region.

ABOVE *A Victorian town has been re-created within Blists Hill open-air museum, complete with post office, foundry, bank, fairground and a photographer's shop where visitors can have their portrait taken*

LEFT *Now a scene of rural calm and great beauty, Ironbridge was a hub of industry in the 18th and 19th centuries, when factories and furnaces belched out smoke*

Oxford

Synonymous with dreaming spires and gilded youth, Oxford is home to one of the world's greatest universities, whose architecturally magnificent buildings dominate the city centre. As early as the 12th century, rich bishops founded colleges, each a self-contained entity whose chapels, libraries, halls and student accommodation were arranged round a central quadrangle. Today, there are 35 colleges, mainly grouped around the ancient High Street, and each with its own character and traditions.

It's perhaps the older foundations that are the most evocative, including 14th-century New College, whose

buildings were the template for every collegiate design thereafter, and the sublime 15th-century complex of Magdalen, complete with Gothic cloister and its own deer park. In contrast to the restraint of these earlier foundations, grandiose structures by some of England's finest architects, such as James Gibbs' Radcliffe Camera (1737–48), Christopher Wren's Sheldonian Theatre (1663), Nicholas Hawksmoor's Clarendon Building (1712) and the Bodleian Library, a wonderful resource spread across several buildings, provide an emphatic pointer to the historic wealth of the University.

BELOW *All Souls' College was founded in 1414 to commemorate those killed in the Hundred Years' War. Its pinnacled North Quad was designed by Hawksmoor in 1716*

RIGHT *The Encaenia Procession en route to the Sheldonian Theatre in June. Here, the Encaenia ceremony awards honorary degrees to distinguished men and women, and dates in its present form from 1760*

BELOW RIGHT *Regarded as a masterpiece of the Palladian style, the Radcliffe Camera is a perfectly circular building built to house a science library and now accommodating a reading room of the Bodleian Library*

Shakespeare Country

ABOVE *Shakespeare's wife, Anne Hathaway, grew up in this cottage, situated on the fringes of woodland. A garden in a field beside the cottage is planted with trees mentioned in Shakespeare's plays*

OPPOSITE *Serenely sited by the banks of the Avon, Shakespeare was baptised and buried at Holy Trinity Church. Dating from 1210, it is Stratford-upon-Avon's oldest building*

Stratford-upon-Avon is a magnet for thousands of visitors annually, who flock here to honour the memory of playwright and poet William Shakespeare, born in the town in 1564.

Without the benefit of the Shakespeare connection, the town would be an unassuming and pleasant market centre standing on the banks of the River Avon, and blessed with a clutch of attractive 16th- and 17th-century buildings. Among them is Harvard House, an ornate high street residence built by the grandfather of John Harvard, the founder of Harvard University, Massachusetts. Other houses in the town centre are associated with the great playwright, and it's these that most visitors come to see. The presence of the Royal Shakespeare Company, housed in two modern riverside theatres, ensures Stratford's pre-eminence on the provincial cultural scene.

William Shakespeare, the son of a glove-maker and a farmer's daughter from Wilmcote, was born in a half-timbered house set back from the river. In 1582, he married Anne Hathaway, who was brought up at nearby Shottery. He left her, and his children, for the bright lights of London, returning to Stratford in 1597, when he purchased a house known as New Place. He died here in 1616, leaving his daughter Susanna comfortably ensconced at nearby Hall's Croft. All these buildings, and their surrounding gardens, are now Shakespeare shrines. Another is the town's handsome Church of the Holy Trinity, whose register records the playwright's death, and whose chancel holds his remains. His gravestone is inscribed:
'Good frend for Jesus sake forbeare/To digg the dust encloased heare/Bleste be ye man yt spares thes stones/And curst be he yt moves my bones.'

ABOVE *Cloister Court in Queens'
College dates from the 15th century,
and is the only courtyard in
Cambridge with such a show
of half-timbering*

RIGHT *The soaring fan vaulting
and sumptuous stained glass of
King's College are the backdrop for
performances by the famous chapel
choir, whose Christmas Eve carol
service is broadcast worldwide*

Cambridge

The compact university city of Cambridge stands on the southern edge of the East Anglian fens, a golden backwater of majestic college buildings and narrow streets, embraced by the curving River Cam and the famous college Backs.

Cambridge is ancient indeed. Nothing remains of its Roman origins, but the castle mound and the Round Church are survivals from the Norman period. The University was founded in 1209, when the first scholars fled here from Oxford, and the colleges were largely established between the 14th and 16th centuries. They usually consist of a hall, chapel, library and student accommodation grouped round a central courtyard, approached through an often magnificent gatehouse. These front the main streets of the town, but the colleges are seen at their best from the Backs, a swathe of green land beside the River Cam, and synonymous with idyllic punting afternoons.

The University has educated outstanding writers, philosophers and statesmen. Trinity's alumni include Byron, Tennyson, William Thackeray and Bertrand Russell, as well as a trio of royals, including Prince Charles, and the Cambridge spies Blunt, Burgess and Philby. It's the biggest college, with the largest courtyard, but the architectural prize goes to King's College. Founded by Henry IV in 1441, its lofty, fan-vaulted chapel is one of Europe's greatest Gothic buildings.

BELOW *Punts make their way beneath Queens' College's Mathematical Bridge. This quintessential way of enjoying the Cam is harder than it looks, and keeping a straight line is a real challenge*

Wool Towns of East Anglia

Suffolk and Essex retain hidden corners that have been largely by-passed by modern times. They reveal beautifully preserved small market towns whose medieval wealth owes much to wool, such as Lavenham, or more esoteric luxuries like saffron, whose cultivation gave Saffron Walden its name. Highly valued for its medicinal properties, as a dye and for culinary purposes, the saffron crocus was grown on a huge scale, surrounding the town with sheets of pale purple during the flowering season.

Wool and saffron merchants, often self-made men, used their wealth to build, erecting splendid half-timbered houses and glorious light-drenched churches. Anxious to steal a march on the less well-to-do, the most prosperous men decorated the plasterwork of their houses with lavish pargetting, a process where the lime plaster within the timber frame is incised or moulded. Pargetting can be simple and low key, or immensely elaborate, with patterns changing from town to town and county to county.

Craftsmen worked the plaster as it dried, using stippling, dragging and combing techniques or stamping designs and raising borders using special moulds and wooden blocks. Grander buildings were decorated with swags, cartouches and friezes, borrowing designs from France, Italy and the Low Countries. The custom survives, and modern houses are still pargetted throughout these eastern counties.

Towns rich in timber-framed, thatched houses include Long Melford, Suffolk, which gets its name from its lengthy main street. Lined with splendid houses, this ends with a flourish at a wide, sloping green, where the solid stone and flint bulk of the church of Holy Trinity stands guard over a row of 16th-century almshouses.

Further down the Stour Valley the market town of Sudbury made its money through silk-weaving. It is more famous as the birthplace of Thomas Gainsborough (1727–88), England's leading 18th-century portraitist. Gainsborough's House displays a collection of his work.

ABOVE *The pargetting on the Old Sun Inn, Saffron Walden, once used by Oliver Cromwell as his headquarters, is among the finest and most ambitious in Essex*

TOP RIGHT *Little Hall, built in the 15th century, stands surrounded by a range of other notable timber-framed houses on Lavenham's spacious triangular Market Place*

RIGHT AND OPPOSITE LEFT *Lavenham's heritage of timber-framed architecture is extraordinarily rich and varied, with styles of timbering and the use of colour wash meaning no two houses are quite alike*

Norwich and the Norfolk Broads

ABOVE *Bishop Herbert de Losinga built Norwich Cathedral in about 1100. Its spire of 315ft (96m) was added by Bishop Goldwell after a fire destroyed the original in 1463*

Sections of medieval walls still surround the heart of Norwich, Norfolk's county town, where ancient churches jostle with merchants' houses whose architecture ranges from timber-framed late medieval to serene Georgian. Rising over the narrow lanes that thread through the city are two landmarks: the creamy stone bulk of the Norman castle, and the slender spire of the cathedral, founded and first built by the Normans and embellished with decorative stonework and woodcarving over the centuries.

This evocative old city was home to the artist John Crome (1768–1821), whose paintings were inspired by the Norfolk Broads, a shifting, watery landscape to the northeast. The Broads are England's largest wetland,

covering 220 square miles (570sq km), and the shallow lakes or broads were formed in the Middle Ages as a result of peat digging. Dykes and wind pumps once controlled the waters. Today they are managed by the Broads Authority, which seeks to balance tourism and recreation with the need to preserve the ecology of this unique eco-system.

Summer sees the rivers and lakes of the Broads packed with sailing boats, canoes and launches, but there are still vast stretches of marsh and reed where nature comes first. Hickling Broad and Horsey Mere are just two of the wildlife preserves where otters swim, bitterns boom and visitors may be lucky enough the spot the meandering flight of the swallowtail butterfly.

ABOVE *The striking stone bulk of the Norman castle commands a view over the city from a hill. It contains a museum and paintings from the Norwich School of Artists*

LEFT *Norwich is home to the colourful stalls of England's largest open-air market, its Market Place surrounded by a range of civic buildings such as Norwich Guildhall*

103

ABOVE AND BELOW *Pumping
mills such as Thurne Mill were
erected to drain the farmland
and to control the levels of the
waterways and are still a
distinctive Broads feature*

LEFT *Barton Broad and the area's other shallow lakes are not natural, but are the result of peat digging in centuries past*

RIGHT *The ideal way to experience the watery landscapes of the Norfolk Broads, such as that at Ranworth shown here, is by boat, whether by yacht, cruiser or canoe*

ABOVE *At Hunstanton, strikingly striped red and white chalk cliffs are rich in fossils, many of which can be found amid cliff falls on the beach*

LEFT *Holkham Hall, a magnificent 18th-century mansion within a huge park adorned by a lake and a classical temple, was home to the agricultural innovator Thomas Coke*

North Norfolk

The coastal lands of North Norfolk stretch beneath huge skies, a patchwork of vast beaches, shingle spits, salt marshes and dunes, backed by tranquil countryside that boasts a clutch of England's finest country houses. There are windmills, round church towers and buildings with distinctive Dutch gables.

Holkham, the home of the Coke family and Earls of Leicester, is a superb Palladian mansion built by Thomas Coke between 1734 and 1761 to house the art collection he had amassed during a European tour. The Holkham estate extends towards an immense beach and the town of Wells, centred round a green lined with elegant Georgian houses. Wells is one of the few places along this northern coast with a sheltered harbour, and was once a major port. Nearby Blakeney boasts wide, windswept beaches.

West of Wells lies Hunstanton, where crumbling cliffs display horizontal stripes of red, white and brown rock strata. The little town was transformed in the 19th century by the coming of the railway, and grew into a seaside resort.

A few miles south, at Heacham, the land is transformed every July into a sea of blue when the acres of lavender surrounding the village bloom. The Norfolk lavender industry was started in the early 1930s by local nurseryman Linn Chilvers. Among the many products of this industry is an intense lavender perfume first made for George IV; its formula remains a closely guarded secret.

BELOW *Lavender fields spread around the village of Heacham and make a spectacular show in summer. The well-drained soil and dry Norfolk climate provide the ideal growing conditions*

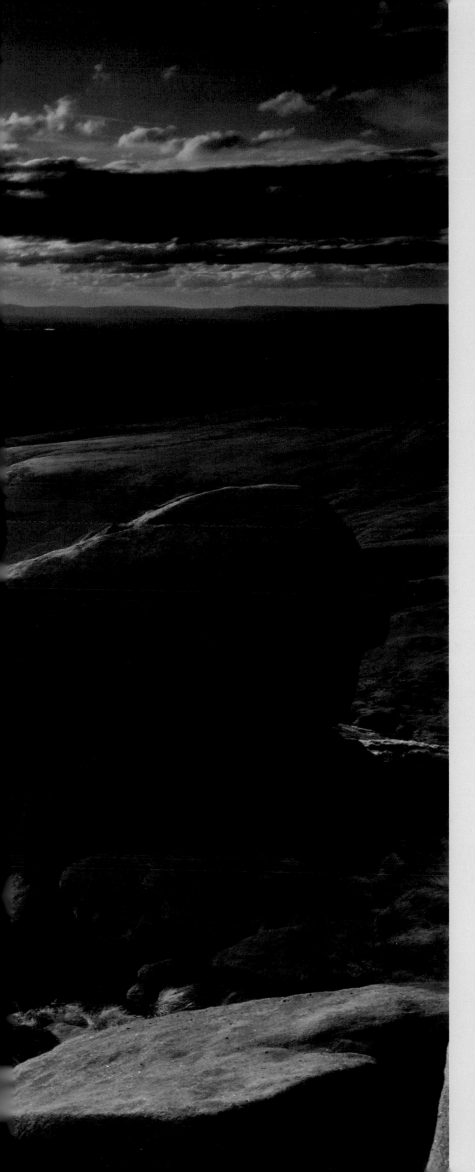

Northern England

The northern counties contain some of England's biggest cities, the crucible in which burned the white-hot fires of the 19th-century Industrial Revolution. Manchester, Leeds, Sheffield and Newcastle upon Tyne have each undergone appreciable renaissances in recent years, but they remain huge urban conglomerations, in which around half of England's population lives and works. In contrast are three cathedral cities that harbour an abundance of history – York, with the finest medieval townscape in Britain, Chester with its remarkably intact town walls, and Durham, with its stupendous cathedral towering high above a loop in the River Wear.

These urban centres are balanced by some of England's most beautiful countryside, a glorious mix of hills, valleys, lakes, rivers and coastal splendour, which provide both an escape for the city dwellers and a livelihood for those who still farm and fish.

As early as the 1950s, five areas were protected by National Park status. The Pennine hills are what is often called the backbone of England, and encompass the National Parks of the Peak District, the Yorkshire Dales and Northumberland. In the northwest corner, the Lake District National Park is perhaps the most cherished of all English landscapes and changes quite astonishingly in mood from one valley to the next, while east of the Pennines the North York Moors National Park extends to North Yorkshire's cliff-fringed coast.

Boulders fringe the windswept heights of
Kinder Scout in the Peak District. In 1932,
ramblers mounted a mass trespass here in a bid
to gain public access to the open moors

The Peak District

Ringed by industrial towns and cities, the Peak District is a strikingly rural enclave of moor and dale at the southern tip of the Pennine Hills and provides the link between the harsh northern uplands and the softer green south. Since 1951, the 555 square miles (1,437sq km) that comprise its two sections – the limestone White Peak to the south, and the millstone grit Dark Peak around its northern, western and eastern edges – have been a National Park, providing a precious oasis of unspoiled countryside in the heavily populated and industrialised north. The high, dry plateaux of the Peak District have been inhabited since earliest times, and many hilltops have Bronze Age burial mounds or barrows (known locally as 'lows'), while stone circles such as the Nine Ladies at Stanton Moor bear witness to the religious rites of ancient civilisations. As the Romans moved north in the second century, the native people retreated to the high tops, building hillforts such as those above the Hope valley at Mam Tor, and leaving the invaders to exploit the Peak's mineral wealth, mining lead that was to remain a major source of revenue in the area right through to the 19th century.

Throughout the Peak District, small towns and villages that once depended on mining and agriculture today serve the park's visitors. One such place is Bakewell, an old town on the River Wye, where narrow streets and stone cottages contrast with the Georgian splendour of Bath Square – the sole remnant of an attempt to develop the town as a fashionable spa in the 18th century. West of here, Buxton thrived on the reputation of its springs, and its elegant crescents and grandiose buildings are the backdrop for a renowned arts and music festival each July.

ABOVE LEFT *Flaky almond-flavoured Bakewell Pudding, on sale in the town, was invented by chance in 1860, when a cook's strawberry tart went wrong; the recipe remains a secret*

ABOVE *Solomon's Temple, near Buxton, is a folly erected in 1896 on the site of a ancient burial site where Bronze Age skeletons have been found*

OPPOSITE *Mam Tor, near Castleton, is known as the 'shivering mountain' because of its many landslips. From its summit extends this exhilarating ridge path*

ABOVE *Curbar Edge is one of the Peak District's distinctive gritstone edges. For centuries, this hard, abrasive stone was used for making millstones*

LEFT ABOVE *Wooded parkland, designed in the 1750s by 'Capability' Brown and bisected by the River Derwent, surrounds Chatsworth House, the country seat of the Dukes of Devonshire*

LEFT *Grey-stone farmhouses throughout the Peak are home to families whose living has been dependent for centuries on the price of wool*

To the northeast, the pretty village of Castleton, ringed by hills and rich in sturdy cottages, draws walkers to the routes that fan out from here – including up to Mam Tor at 1,696ft (517m), the second highest peak in the park. Other visitors head underground to explore the limestone cave systems near by; two of these (Blue John and Treak Cliff) were mined for Blue John, a mauve outcrop found only in this area and still used for making jewellery and ornaments.

Mining, quarrying and wool production filled the coffers of the Peak's great landowner, the Duke of Devonshire, who erected the great house of Chatsworth near Bakewell. Chatsworth was built on the site of a former Elizabethan manor as a grand classical house between 1687 and 1707 by William Cavendish, the 1st Duke. Packed with exceptional paintings and furniture, Chatsworth's State Rooms spread in splendour along the whole length of the south front, which overlooks the formal gardens and the vast park.

There are lower-key architectural pleasures at Haddon Hall, a mellow grey-stone medieval house to the south that was sensitively restored in the 1930s by the Peak's other great lord, the Duke of Rutland.

For the majority of visitors, it's the outdoor opportunities that are the main draw. Some tracks head for the barren, peat-covered moorland of the Dark Peak, while others wend their way through limestone gorges such as Monsal Dale and across the patchwork of stone-walled fields of the White Peak.

ABOVE *The majestic Derwent Valley Reservoirs form the largest body of open water in the Peak District and supply cities such as Nottingham, Derby and Sheffield*

Liverpool

The city of Liverpool stands at the mouth of the River Mersey, still the largest port for trade with the USA's eastern seaboard. Liverpool's first docks were built in 1715, and for the next century, the city was Europe's major slave port. From here, textiles, alcohol and weaponry were traded to Africa for slaves, who were shipped to the Caribbean in exchange for tobacco, cotton and sugar for the British markets. After the abolition of slavery, Liverpool's main export was still people, but this time it was 9 million emigrants from all over Europe passing through on their way to the New World and Australia between 1830 and 1930. The city's own population grew five-fold as immigrants from China, the Caribbean and Ireland flooded in, making Liverpool one of Britain's earliest multi-ethnic communities, with a vibrancy that survived the late 20th-century economic downturn.

Liverpool today is experiencing a renaissance, with new jobs being created and urban regeneration high on the agenda. The dockland area, with its museums and upmarket bars and shops, is thriving, the arts scene buzzing, and a newly confident city emerged following its role as European Capital of Culture in 2008.

The traditional pleasures are still there. Liverpool has some fine architecture, with two stylistically contrasting cathedrals (the Anglican Cathedral Church of Christ and the Catholic Liverpool Metropolitan Cathedral) and imposing Victorian and Edwardian civic buildings that house museums devoted to everything from Liverpool life to superb collections of art. The waterside, dominated by the iconic Liver Building and the Port of Liverpool Building, has found a new role since the redevelopment of the Albert Dock. This features a museum devoted to Liverpool's most famous sons, the Beatles.

LEFT *The main waterfront buildings are known as the Three Graces. The Royal Liver Building is topped by the 'Liver Birds' – two bronze mythical birds that have become the city's symbol*

ABOVE *Liverpool's Metropolitan Cathedral of Christ the King was built in the 1960s. Its brilliant stained glass bathes the interior with light*

TOP *A statue of John Lennon stands outside the Cavern Club, where the Beatles first made their name in 1961 and launched their rise to fame*

The Yorkshire Dales

Along the backbone of the Pennine hills, the Yorkshire Dales National Park encompasses a series of valleys that epitomise rural Yorkshire. They form a varied landscape of high limestone and gritstone hills and pastoral valleys, characterised by dry-stone walls and stone barns, traditionally used for storing hay and housing cattle. Domestic buildings have a striking uniformity: many bear gritstone lintels, mullions, cornerstones and doorheads, beneath sturdy flagstone roofs.

Most of the dales take their names from the rivers that run through them, starting with Swaledale and Wensleydale in the north and spreading south to Wharfedale, Ribblesdale and Malhamdale. These three are easily reached from the market town of Settle, the terminus for the Settle-to-Carlisle railway line, 72 miles (116km) long, justly promoted as England's most scenic railway.

ABOVE *Rich grazing pastures abound in the Dales, where the fields are enclosed by dry-stone walls and dotted with traditional stone barns such as these in Wensleydale*

RIGHT *Kilnsey Crag, Wharfedale, attracts climbers challenged by its glacially carved overhang. At its foot, the still waters of a trout farm provide gentler amusement*

Swaledale is rich in settlements with Norse names – such as Thwaite, Keld, Reeth, Angram and Muker – and the Vikings have left their legacy too, in the traditional laithes, predecessors of the ancient field barns that still dot the pasture today. Found all over the Dales, they are particularly numerous around here.

Swaledale is approached from the east through Richmond, a gem of a town on the River Swale. Richmond is overshadowed by the massive walls and keep of a Norman castle, high on a rocky promontory, in which is preserved Scolland's Hall, which claims to be the most ancient great hall in England. Elsewhere in the town, the accent is Georgian, with attractive old buildings lining the streets that lead off from the spacious, cobbled market square. The little Georgian theatre dates from 1788, and is the oldest in the country.

To the south, Malhamdale is classic limestone countryside, dominated by the massive vertical cliffs of Malham Cove. This remarkable feature was created during the Ice Age, and is topped by a limestone pavement prized

ABOVE *The Dales are rich in limestone cliffs and turbulent rivers as here, where the River Swale drops suddenly at Wainwath Falls*

for its rare flora that grows within the cracks, known as grykes. Close by is Gordale Scar, where a waterfall swirls through a chasm at the top of a wildly rugged valley. The village of Malham lies on the Pennine Way, a trail that runs 256 miles (412km) from Edale in the Peak District to the Scottish Borders. In Yorkshire, it takes in dramatic landscapes that include Pen-y-ghent, which makes up the Three Peaks, along with Whernside and Ingleborough, easily identified by its flat top. This is cave and pothole country; two local caves to visit are Ingleborough Cave and White Scar Cave, which features an underground waterfall. At Ingleton, a trail leads past the Ingleton Waterfalls, through the gorges of the rivers Twiss and Doe.

There's more thundering water after rain at Hardraw Force, England's highest waterfall, which is located near Wensleydale's main hiking centre, Hawes. The market town is home to the crumbly white Wensleydale cheese, first made here in medieval times by Cistercian monks. The village of Wensley, attractively set round a tiny square, boasts the Dales' best-preserved medieval church, Holy Trinity, which dates back to the 13th century. Its main rival in the area is St Andrew's at Aysgarth, renowned for its three falls of water cascading over a series of broad limestone platforms just outside the village on the road to Carperby.

ABOVE *Hardraw Force, the highest single-drop waterfall in England, can only be reached by passing through the Green Dragon Inn at the hamlet of Hardraw*

LEFT *Amid rowan trees and bracken on moorland, Brimham Rocks comprise a great number of stacks of resilient millstone grit that have been carved over millennia by the elements*

RIGHT *The recipe for crumbly, mild Wensleydale cheese is thought to have originated with French monks and handed down through farmers' families. It is still made in Hawes*

OPPOSITE *The grykes (fissures) and clints (blocks) of this natural pavement form part of an extraordinary geological wonderland around Malham Cove*

York

York's long history dates back to Roman times, when it was the northern capital of *Eboracum*, but its modern name derives from its 9th-century Danish name, *Jorvik*. The city was capital of the Danelaw, and the Viking legacy is still evident in its street names and the treasures in its museums. The Danes were driven out in 1066, and the real glories of York, including its superbly preserved city walls, date from medieval times.

Chief among these is the Minster, England's largest medieval cathedral and seat of the Archbishop of York.

It was constructed over a period of 250 years from 1260. The immense nave is lit by windows containing some of England's best medieval stained glass, notably in the majestic East Window.

South of the Minster, the cramped, narrow streets of the Shambles, lined with timber-framed houses, perfectly characterise the old city, while scattered throughout old York are a further 18 medieval churches. The pleasures of the modern city include a vibrant cultural scene and the lure of the York Racecourse.

RIGHT *The pinnacled western towers of York Minster, one of Europe's largest Gothic cathedrals, contain bells that chime on the quarter hour*

OPPOSITE *The old houses and shops of The Shambles were built so close that it is possible to shake hands with the opposite occupant across the street from the top windows*

44
CHOCOLATE HEAVEN
Handmade Chocolates
CHOCOLATE HEAVEN
W. HAMOND
YORK
silverado
GUEST WALKER & CO
PAST IMAGES

North York Moors

Running from the Hambleton and Cleveland hills in the west to the dramatic cliffs of the coast in the east, the North York Moors are flat-topped, heather-clad expanses cut by deep green valleys, interrupted towards the east by large patches of modern forestry, dotted with villages of wide-verged streets lined with cottages with yellow limestone walls and red pantiled roofs. The area has been inhabited ever since the neolithic period and successive waves of settlers have left their mark in the shape of barrows and hillforts, Roman remains and the evocative ruins of the great monastic foundations that flourished here in the medieval period.

Now enclosed within the borders of a National Park, the moors offer exhilarating walking, notably along the Cleveland Way (110 miles/177km), which takes a horseshoe route along the escarpments and down the coastal clifftops. On the western moors, the steep incline of Sutton Bank, near a hill carving of a white horse created by a local schoolmaster and his pupils in 1857, provides grandstand views across to the Pennines.

Helmsley lies close to the substantial ruins of the Cistercian Rievaulx Abbey, once the area's major landowner. The Rievaulx Terraces were built in the spirit of 18th-century Romanticism to enhance the abbey views.

LEFT *Rievaulx Abbey, one of a number of imposing monastic ruins in the area, occupies a beautiful setting in the valley of the River Rye*

BELOW *A monument on the moors commemorates Captain Cook, whose seafaring career began in Whitby and who spent his childhood at a farm near by*

BELOW RIGHT *The village of Staithes has changed remarkably little over the years. Fishermen still use the traditional craft known as cobles*

North of here, the wild heights of the North York Moors rise up – remote-feeling country scattered with ancient crosses and standing stones; this is the largest tract of continuous heather moor in England, and is a blaze of purple in summer. The loveliest village in the area is Hutton-le-Hole, whose village green, dissected by a stream, is dotted with grazing sheep. It's close to the deep, secretive valleys of Rosedale and Farndale. In spring, thousands come to Farndale to walk through the vast spreads of golden wild daffodils that grow along the banks of the River Dove between Low Mill and Church Houses.

The appealing old market town of Pickering is the starting point for exploring the eastern moors. It is also the home of the volunteer-run, preserved North Yorkshire Moors Railway – one of its steam engines starred as the *Hogwarts Express* in the Harry Potter films. The line runs to Grosmont, a village in leafy Esk Dale, whose river reaches the sea at Whitby.

Between Whitby and Pickering stretches Dalby Forest, an expanse of moorland and conifer plantations. Its bleakness is redeemed by the charms of Thornton-le-Dale, where a shallow brook winds past immaculately tended gardens, and a slender, stepped market cross and stocks stand by the village green.

The North Yorkshire Coast

Whitby is a gem, a bustling fishing port and resort, forever associated with Bram Stoker's gothic novel *Dracula* (1897). The town was a major centre of learning in the early Christian period, its abbey hosting the seminally important Synod of Whitby in 664, which decided the method for calculating the date of Easter.

Cobbled Church Street is lined with shops selling the local jet jewellery, whose manufacture was once a major local industry. From its seaward end, 199 steps climb up to the hilltop Church of St Mary, founded in the 12th century, giving great views over the harbour below. Above the other bank of the Esk, a whalebone arch commemorating Whitby's past whaling industry frames a view of the abbey.

From Whitby, the Cleveland Way runs north along the coast to the fishing village of Staithes, a huddle of stone houses around a harbour protected from the wild northerly winds by the bright red sandstone outcrop of Cowbar Nab.

Durham

The physical presence of this compact historic city is unlike any other in Britain. On a lofty site protected by sandstone cliffs bounded at their base by a tight meander of the River Wear, stands the Norman cathedral, featuring the shrine of St Cuthbert of Lindisfarne. Built in a relatively brief period from 1070 to 1140, the cathedral has a superb sense of architectural cohesion, and features what is believed to be the Britain's earliest use of pointed Gothic arches as well as the rounded arches that preceded them. Its gracious precincts incorporate College Green, where some of the buildings date from the Middle Ages and constitute the most complete example of a Benedictine monastery in the country, which includes cloisters, a chapter house, the former prior's kitchen and a library.

The cathedral fronts on to Palace Green along with the buildings of the university. These include the castle, which dates from the 11th century and was built as the residence for the Bishop of Durham. The rest of the old town is easily seen on foot, with attractive 18th-century houses lining cobbled South Bailey and North Bailey, and in the Market Place is a lively Saturday market that has been held since medieval times.

The Lake District

Tucked within an area measuring a mere 30 miles (48km), this area displays extraordinary diversity and bewitching beauty. From a central volcanic dome comprising the highest group of mountains, or fells, a series of valleys radiate. These feature the area's 16 lakes, all formed after the last Ice Age as meltwater was dammed by terminal moraine. The landscape changes abruptly according to the rock type, with gnarled, craggy volcanic fells at the centre and to the west, green and smooth slatey slopes to the north and gentler limestone hills to the southeast.

For centuries this was regarded as remote, hard country, its scenic grandeur viewed with awe by all but its own people. Attitudes changed at the end of the 18th century with the start of the Romantic Movement, which bought painters and poets such as John Constable and William Wordsworth to the area. Taken by its breathtaking splendour, they celebrated the sheer variety of its landscape in art and writing and attracted the high-spending visitors who could no longer indulge in Grand Tours on a European mainland torn by the Napoleonic Wars. It was the start of the British love affair with the great outdoors – an affair that, over the last two hundred years, has brought town dwellers not only to the Lakes, but also to every other wild corner of the British Isles.

The Lakes Today

The Lake District today is a National Park, attracting millions of visitors annually, who come to relax around the lakes and potter in the villages, or boot up and head for the hills. Happily, most of them concentrate on specific areas, so it's still possible to experience the unspoiled beauty that attracted the first travellers.

Boat services make a memorable way to enjoy Windermere, Ullswater, Derwent Water and Coniston Water, and other highlights include the breathtaking drive along the Hardknott and Wrynose passes, the Langdale, valleys and the villages of Hawkshead and Grasmere, once home to Wordsworth and his diarist sister, Dorothy.

An unmissable Lakeland experience is to walk one of the superb horseshoe routes along the high ridges such as up to Helvellyn via Striding Edge, or to hike in the majestic areas to the west around Crummock Water, Buttermere and lonely Wast Water, backed by the peaks of the Great Gable and Scafell Pike.

TOP *William Wordsworth and his wife Mary are buried here at St Oswald's Church in Grasmere, close to the graves of their children and his sister Dorothy*

ABOVE *Dove Cottage, originally a pub, was one of several local houses where William Wordsworth lived. He spent his most productive years as a poet here, from 1799 to 1808*

LEFT *Windermere, England's longest natural lake, is the area's prime boating spot, with all sorts of craft in evidence. A steamer plies the length of the lake*

OVER *A view from the Skiddaw range over Keswick and Derwent Water. In the 19th century, when the Lakes began to attract tourists in large numbers, Skiddaw was the peak of choice for the best views*

ABOVE *A beck flows under tiny Ashness Bridge, with its backdrop of island-speckled Derwent Water and the slatey, green slopes of Skiddaw beyond*

INSIDE *The Great Langdale valley in the Lake District opens up in spectacular fashion to a frieze of snowy mountain peaks*

RIGHT *Castlerigg Stone Circle, above Keswick, is a late neolithic site, probably erected around 3000BC for ceremonial purposes. It comprises 38 stones enclosing a rectangle of a further 10 stones*

LEFT *Herdwick sheep are the hardiest British hill sheep breed and can survive the Lake District winters. They are found on the central and western fells, such as here at Loughrigg Fell, looking into the Langdale Valley*

BELOW *Even the smallest of lakes offer beautiful views, such as here at Blea Tarn, located between Little Langdale Valley and Dungeon Ghyll*

The Northumberland Coast

Peaceful under the summer sun but wild and treacherous in winter, the Northumberland coast stretches north from Newcastle to the Scottish border. This is Percy country, and two great strongholds bear witness to the power of this northern dukedom. The Percys built the mighty castle at Warkworth in the 14th century, living there for 200 years until moving to their other castle at Alnwick, an imposing pile on the edge of an attractive old town. Remodelled over the centuries, Alnwick Castle pulls in the crowds on the Harry Potter trail – it starred as Hogwarts School in the films – and to the innovative, contemporary Alnwick Garden, with its huge tree house, poison garden and bamboo labyrinth. North from here, tiny villages like

Craster, famed for its kippers, Embleton and Beadnell overlook huge, empty beaches, and there's windy walking out to the ruins of 14th-century Dunstanburgh Castle.

Seahouses is the departure point for the Farne Islands, a rocky archipelago that's home to grey seals and migrating seabirds. Further north, Bamburgh Castle, magnificently set above sweeping sands and rolling surf, was once capital of Northumberland; its present appearance dates from an Edwardian makeover. Huge beaches stretch up the coast, encircling the holy island of Lindisfarne, reached at low tide across a causeway.

LEFT *The 16th-century castle on Holy Island was remodelled by Edwin Lutyens in the early 20th century. Nearby is the priory, where, in around AD700, monks illuminated the manuscript known as the Lindisfarne Gospels*

OPPOSITE *Bamburgh Castle, built on a basalt outcrop, became the Northumbrian capital under King Oswald in the 7th century. Its 12th-century keep has extremely thick walls*

Newcastle upon Tyne

The city of Newcastle burgeoned in the 17th century, when coal export provided the wealth for the development of shipbuilding. Two hundred years later Newcastle was building 25 per cent of the world's ships. Fine civic buildings went up in the Victorian heart of Grainger Town, and the High Level Bridge was constructed over the Tyne, one of a series of eye-catching bridges seen today.

Industrial decline hit in the 1930s and Newcastle became increasingly run down, though its warm-hearted citizens, known as Geordies, remained staunchly loyal and proud of their home. Vindication came in the 1990s, and recent years have seen an extraordinary turnabout, with Newcastle today noted as a vibrant cultural centre with a buzzing night scene. This renaissance is seen particularly in the waterfront areas. To the north, the 16th-century merchants' houses of Quayside contrast with the sleek regeneration of the area beyond the Tyne Bridge – a parade of riverside promenades, squares, apartment buildings, bars and restaurants. Across the river, the Gateshead Quays are home to the huge Baltic Centre for Contemporary Art, within a converted flour mill, and the Sage Gateshead world-class concert venue.

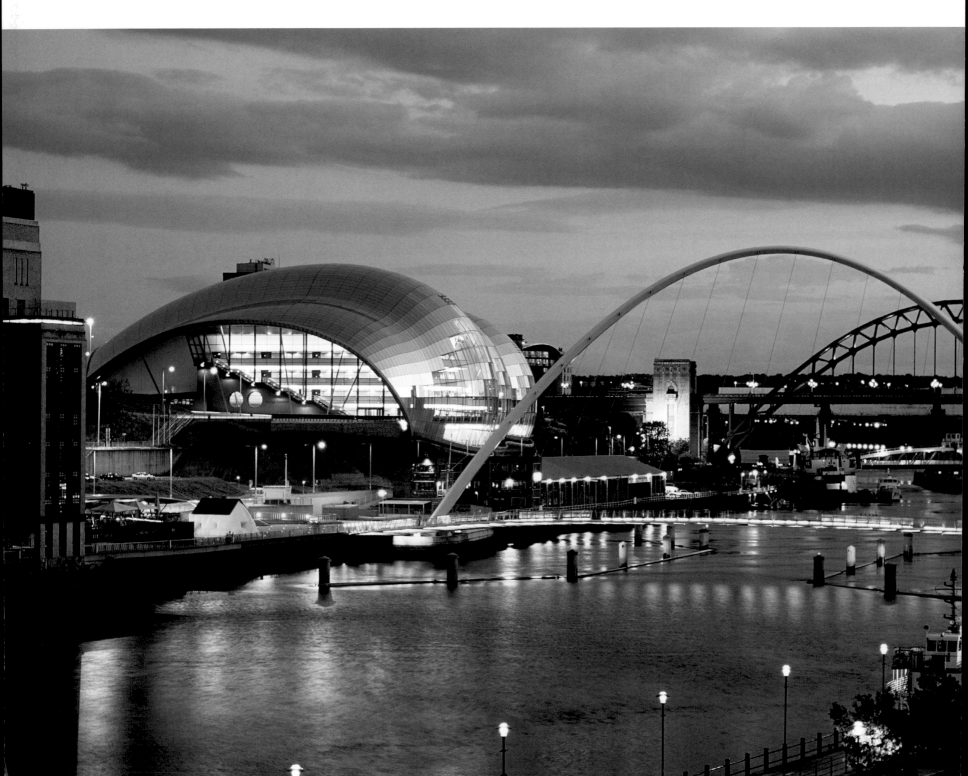

BELOW *Dusk over the Tyne, with the looming Tyne Bridge (1928) in the background and the graceful arch of the Gateshead Millennium Bridge, designed to pivot to allow passage for ships*

ABOVE *Antony Gormley's iconic steel sculpture,* The Angel of the North *(1998), dominates the southern approaches to Newcastle and Gateshead. The sculptor intended it to create 'a sense of embrace'*

RIGHT *Grey's Monument has been a Newcastle landmark since its construction in 1838. It commemorates the passing of the Reform Act by Lord Grey, six years earlier*

Scotland

Over the northern English border lies Scotland, a remote country that packs some of Europe's wildest and most beautiful landscape into its 30,000 square miles (77,700sq km). Its elegant capital is Edinburgh, its largest city Glasgow, and one fifth of its 5 million-strong population live in these two cities. Unified politically with England since 1707, Scotland has always had a problematical relationship with the 'auld enemy'. Despite the establishment in 1999 of the devolved Scottish Parliament, many Scots still view the 'big brother' south of the border with mixed feelings.

The country is defined by its scenery, an intoxicating blend of high mountains and lochs in the north and green hills and fertile rolling farmland in the south, encircled by an intricate coastline, 2,300 miles (3,700km) long, that has few scenic rivals in Europe. When not shrouded in mist and driving rain, this landscape reveals a haunting beauty which is apparent in such elements as its purple heather-cloaked hills and its vivid autumn tints reflected in glassy lochs. Amid this natural wonderland, Scotland's grey stone towns and villages retain their own gritty character, with a spirit that's wholly different from urban life south of the border. Visitors revel in the great outdoors, the ancient castles, the whole tartan and whisky package – but increasingly outsiders are also beginning to see the reality of modern Scotland, a dynamic, self-assured country which has learned to combine its heritage with a culture that looks firmly forward into the 21st century.

The Ring of Brodgar is a truly circular late Neolithic or early Bronze Age stone ring located on the largest island in Orkney. It is part of the UNESCO World Heritage Site known as the Heart of Neolithic Orkney

Edinburgh

Scotland's capital is both a visually captivating, historic city and a thriving, cosmopolitan centre, whose quality of life is rated the highest in Great Britain.

The city's history dates back to the Dark Ages, but it was only in the 15th century that it became the capital of Scotland. When James VI of Scotland became James I of England in 1603, Edinburgh was forced to accept the Union of the Crowns. A further blow was dealt to its prestige a century later, when the Union of the Parliaments, in 1707, saw Scottish independence finally at an end. However, the guaranteed preservation of the national church and the Scottish legal and educational systems ensured the city never completely lost its national identity. Vindication came in the last years of the 20th century with

the establishment of a Scottish parliament and a surge in national confidence.

Today, Edinburgh is a prosperous, slick and stylish city with a level of sophistication undreamed of even 20 years ago; it is at its most exuberant during its world-renowned arts festival in August. The past is still highly visible: the castle still rises majestically over the tall tenements, narrow streets and dark vennels of the Old Town, where the cobbled thoroughfare of the Royal Mile links the 12th-century castle with the 16th-century royal palace of Holyrood, the Queen's official residence in Scotland. Between the two, Gladstone's Land is a historic house marvellously evoking living conditions in an Old Town tenement 400 years ago.

In total contrast, the New Town is an elegant and remarkably complete area of crisply proportioned Georgian architecture. Bounded on the city centre side by Princes Street and the high-Gothic memorial to Sir Walter Scott, this extraordinary development features crescents, squares, a 'circus' and areas of green open space. The area was created during the late 18th and early 19th centuries, when shortage of space and cramped conditions saw the construction of this entirely new suburb.

Uniquely among British cities, Edinburgh has a huge volcanic hill, Holyrood Park, rising close to its centre. Another vantage point is Calton Hill, featuring a monument to philosopher Dugald Stewart and a National Monument, modelled on the Parthenon in Athens.

OPPOSITE *Carved from life, this statue commemorates Bobby, a Skye terrier who kept vigil for 14 years at his master's grave in Greyfriars churchyard from 1858*

BELOW LEFT *Perched on a volcanic crag, Edinburgh Castle rises above Princes Street Gardens. Human settlers came here around 900 BC and the royal fortress dates from the 12th century*

BELOW *Princes Street is one of the city's premier shopping streets, punctuated by the tower of the Balmoral Hotel and the spires of St Marys Episcopal Cathedral*

LEFT *The elegant classical architecture of the New Town is manifested in this 18th-century doorway and fanlight in a stone-fronted house in Queen Street*

LEFT *Fifty thousand tonnes of steel were used in the construction of the Forth Rail Bridge, built across the Firth of Forth to the northwest of Edinburgh between 1883 and 1890. It is a superb example of Victorian engineering*

BELOW AND RIGHT *Completed in 2004 to the design of Enric Miralles, the Scottish Parliament building is one of Scotland's most innovative examples of modern architecture, contrasting with the traditional design of nearby Palace of Holyroodhouse*

Burns Country

The fertile west coast country of Ayrshire will forever be synonymous with Robert Burns (1759–1796), Scotland's much-loved national poet, whose verse continues to strike a note in people's hearts the world over.

Born in Alloway, his early years were marked by his father's poverty as a tenant farmer, an experience that gave him a life-long antipathy towards the land-owning classes. His first volume of poems was published in 1786 and was a best seller. Writing, however, didn't pay the bills and he was never able to abandon the day job, working throughout his short life as first a farmer, and later an exciseman.

Burns was a radical, a nationalist, a wit and a romantic. He was also a great womaniser, and many of his best-known songs celebrate his love for the fairer sex. He wrote always in his native Ayrshire Scots vernacular on familiar themes – celebrating, mourning and raging about life and the hand dealt to the common man. Worn out by hard labour and ill health, he died aged 37. Southwest Scotland draws myriad visitors, who flock to his birthplace in Alloway, Ellisland Farm (where he lived from 1788 to 1791) and his home and burial place in Dumfries.

ABOVE *Robert Burns' portrait appears everywhere in Ayrshire. The image on this pub sign is based on a 1786 portrait by Archibald Skirving*

ABOVE *In the churchyard of ruined Alloway Kirk is Robert Burns' parents' gravestone. Burns set part of his rollicking tale* Tam o' Shanter *here*

RIGHT *Burns' birthplace village of Alloway, seen here from the Brig o'Doon, brings many on the trail of the famous Scottish poet*

OPPOSITE *Culzean Castle, overlooking the Firth of Clyde in Ayrshire, was built in 1777 by the Scots architect Robert Adam and contains some of his finest neoclassical designs*

Glasgow

Scotland's largest city, Glasgow has long since shaken off its downbeat image, the legacy, until the 1980s, of its industrial past. Chartered in 1175, the city evolved into an important university centre and port, and by the late 18th century its position on the River Clyde and easy access to the Lanarkshire coalfields had provided the impetus that transformed it into a Victorian industrial giant and the centre – until the 1930s – of British shipbuilding.

Mercantile and industrial wealth created the city, packed with solid and impressive Victorian buildings and home to a highly individualistic people, who retained their innate values throughout the hard times and depression of the late 20th century. The 1990s saw a complete turnaround, and Glaswegians have seen their city regain its role as a confident metropolis, noted for its unique combination of glitz and grime.

Glasgow has some of the finest 19th-century architecture in Britain, strikingly seen at its best in the art nouveau work of the architect and designer Charles Rennie Mackintosh (1868–1928). It also boasts a clutch of excellent museums, many of them sited around the turreted towers of the university in the city's West End, around peaceful Kelvingrove Park. Elsewhere, there's superb art at the eclectic Burrell Collection, while Glasgow's citizens and everyday life are celebrated at the People's Palace on Glasgow Green. The Glaswegians' love affair with

ABOVE *The Charing Cross fountain epitomises solid Victorian values, hard work and prosperity – all contributed to Glasgow's industrial Golden Age and imposing civic architecture*

'the beautiful game' can be witnessed at Hampden Park, Scotland's national football stadium.

The heart of the city lies on the north bank of the Clyde, centred around the 19th-century municipal showcase of George Square and neighbouring Sauchiehall and Buchanan streets, each a stone's throw from the gentrified grid of 18th-century warehouse streets now revived as the Merchant City.

On the riverside, history meets the ultra-modern in the form of the restored Tall Ship *Glenlee* in Glasgow Harbour, one of the last Clyde-built sailing vessels, and the sleek, titanium-clad Science Centre and Scottish Exhibition Centre.

LEFT *Everything in the Willow Tea Rooms in Sauchiehall Street, from the furniture, china and cutlery to the building itself, was designed by Charles Rennie Mackintosh*

BELOW *On Glasgow's excitingly revived waterfront, the disused Finnieston Crane has been retained as a landmark between the Clyde Auditorium, affectionately nicknamed the Armadillo, and the shapely Clyde Arc road bridge*

LEFT *The huge expanse of Loch Lomond, Britain's largest freshwater lake, is dotted with some 30 islands, some built in prehistoric times*

OPPOSITE *Balmaha, on the eastern shore of Loch Lomond, is often busy with boating activity. Walkers tackling the long-distance West Highland Way pass through the village*

Loch Lomond and the Trossachs

ABOVE *The thistle, Scotland's floral emblem since the 13th century, first appeared as a royal Scottish symbol on the coinage of James III in 1540*

More than 70 per cent of Scotland's population live less than an hour's travel time away from Loch Lomond and the Trossachs, a hugely contrasting area that includes high mountains, lochs, rivers and woodlands. A National Park was created in 2002, stretching from the southern end of Loch Lomond north to Tyndrum and Killin in Perthshire, and east from Callander almost to Loch Fyne.

The area is traversed by the West Highland Way, a spectacular long-distance footpath through some of Scotland's wildest beauty. It follows valley floors, old drove roads, military roads and even disused railways from the outskirts of Glasgow to Fort William in the north.

Within the National Park, the biggest attractions are Loch Lomond itself – the largest expanse of fresh water in Britain – and its attendant mountain, Ben Lomond, at 3,192 feet (973m) the most southerly of Scotland's Munros (the 284 Scottish mountains classified as standing over

3,000 feet (914m). The western banks of Loch Lomond lie just 20 miles (32km) from the centre of Glasgow, drawing myriad weekend visitors. It's easy enough to escape the crowds on the eastern shore, however, and ferries operate to the loch's scattering of islands from the village of Balmaha.

East of Loch Lomond lies the Trossachs, the first region of true Highland grandeur for travellers arriving from the south, and an area first popularised by the writing of Sir Walter Scott (1771–1832) – his novel *Rob Roy* and long poem 'The Lady of the Lake' were both set here. The real Rob Roy, a 17th-century outlaw with a reputation in Scotland to rival that of the legendary Robin Hood in England, was born at Loch Katrine and lived all his life in the Trossachs, turning from life as a respectable farmer to cattle stealing in 1712. His romanticised story, a dramatised illustration of the clash between Gaelic-speaking culture and organised Lowland society, which culminated in the

Jacobite defeat at Culloden in 1746, draws thousands of visitors here each year.

The Trossachs' main towns are Callander, set on the banks of the River Teith at the south end of the Pass of Leny, and Aberfoyle, a sleepy little place packed with holidaymakers in summer. The latter is beautifully set near the forests of Loch Ard and the Queen Elizabeth Forest Park. Idyllic Loch Katrine is only accessible (as it has been since 1900) by a venerable steamer, the SS *Sir Walter Scott*, which chugs through some of the Trossachs' most dramatic and attractive scenery.

North from here the country becomes wilder and less wooded with the start of the true Highlands. Roads are few in this remote region, whose main settlements are the villages of Crianlarich and Tyndrum. The latter was the site of a mini-gold rush in the 19th century, and gold is still occasionally found in the surrounding hills.

West of Loch Lomond itself, Loch Long and the Argyll Forest Park on the Cowal peninsula offer another peaceful taste of this lovely area. Penetrated by the narrow sea lochs of Gare Loch, Loch Long and Loch Fyne, the Cowal offers spectacular hills in the shape of the Arrochar Alps to the north of Loch Long, and utter tranquillity (and views to the lovely island of Arran) along the east shore of Loch Fyne, accessible for part of its length via a narrow single-track road.

ABOVE *Distinctive for their long pelts and long horns, the variously coloured Highland cattle are an ancient breed that can survive in the harsh Scottish climate*

LEFT *Queen Victoria once stayed by Loch Achray at this former hotel, built in the style of a Scottish castle and now converted into holiday apartments*

OPPOSITE *The steep pass at the head of Glen Croe on the Cowal peninsula was named Rest and be thankful by exhausted early travellers*

Mull

The second largest of the Inner Hebrides, Mull is traditionally a crofting, fishing and distilling island. It lies across the Firth of Lorne from Oban, a busy harbour town on Scotland's West Highland coast. Its 19th-century population of 10,000 has dwindled to 3,000, but in Highland terms Mull is a success story, with a growing population of settlers from outside, drawn by the prospect of a peaceful way of life in unspoiled countryside.

Mull displays strikingly diversity, with scenery that ranges from sometimes bleak, undulating tracts of moor and bog, to its highest point, Ben More at 3,169 feet (966m), an extinct volcano. The coastline, particularly to the west, is one of its greatest assets; white sand beaches around Calgary contrast with soaring cliffs at Loch na Keal, a deep indentation that almost bisects the island. North of here is the capital, Tobermory. The road south leads via pastoral Salen to Craignure, the main ferry port, and the castles of Torosay and Duart. From Craignure, a lonely road crosses the Ross of Mull to Fionnphort, the jumping off point for Iona and the magical island of Staffa, with its black basalt columns that inspired Felix Mendelssohn's overture *The Hebrides* (1830).

RIGHT *Torosay Castle near Craignure was built in the Scottish Baronial style in 1858. Its grounds include a beautiful garden and formal terraces*

BELOW *The rugged shores of Loch na Keal on Mull, are divided from Loch Tuath by the islands of Ulva and Gometra*

ABOVE *An abandoned fishing boat stands on a deserted shore near the tiny harbour at Croig on Mull's intricate coast, west of Tobermory*

RIGHT *A solitary cottage stands beneath the formidable slopes of Ben More, on Mull, the only 'Munro' on a Scottish island other than Skye*

FAR RIGHT *A lawn spreads in front of Torosay Castle, designed in Scottish Baronial style by David Bryce and completed in 1858. The narrow-gauge Isle of Mull Railway connects it with Craignure*

OVER *Otters are seen frequently around the shores of Mull; here, a female otter appears from among seaweed*

ABOVE *A view towards Iona from Mull's low-lying shores, fringed with rocks and sparkling white sand beaches formed by the ceaseless grinding action of the water on shells*

RIGHT *Originally a timber monastery, Iona Abbey was rebuilt in stone around 1200 by the Benedictines, attacked by Vikings and left derelict after the Reformation in 1560*

INSIDE *The brightly coloured houses of Tobermory, founded in 1788 as a fishing port, cluster round a sheltered harbour in the north of Mull*

Iona

Set like a jewel in clear blue waters, the holy island of Iona lies less than a mile off the southwestern tip of Mull. It was here, in AD563, that St Columba landed after his flight from Ireland, establishing a monastery whose monks spearheaded the conversion of pagan Scotland and much of northern England. The religion they taught was Celtic Christianity, and through the 6th and 7th centuries the monastery on Iona became a powerhouse of sacred learning and artistic endeavour. Its most famous illuminated manuscript, the *Book of Kells*, is on display in Trinity College, Dublin.

Viking raids and the relentless march of Rome led to the demise of the Celtic church, and by the 13th century Iona was part of mainstream Christianity, with a Benedictine monastery and Augustinian convent.

Both were destroyed during the Reformation, along with all but three of the island's 360 magnificent Celtic crosses, and Iona remained a backwater until 1899, when the abbey church was restored. In 1938, Glasgow minister George MacLeod established the Iona Community, which has evolved from a strictly male, Gaelic-speaking community into a vibrant, internationally renowned ecumenical society.

The heart of Iona is the sensitively restored Abbey, originally constructed by the Benedictines in the 13th century. It stands just north of the island's oldest building, St Oran's Chapel, and Reilig Odhráin (Oran's cemetery), an ancient burial ground said to contain the graves of 60 kings of Scotland, Ireland, Norway and France. Many of its exquisite carved stones have been moved for safe keeping, but St Martin's Cross, an 8th-century Celtic high cross, smothered in figurative carving, still stands outside the abbey church on the ancient and magnificently preserved cobbled Street of the Dead. By the pier are remains of a nunnery.

BELOW *The cloisters lie on the north side of Iona Abbey, where running water was available, rather than the traditional south side*

The East Neuk

From Largo Bay, on the north shore of the Firth of Forth, a string of coastal villages runs along the East Neuk, the name given to this southeastern corner of Fife. Historically prosperous from fishing and trade, it was aptly described in the 15th century by James II as 'the golden fringe on the beggar's mantle' of his poverty-stricken kingdom.

They still fish from the cosy stone harbours of Crail, Anstruther, Pittenweem, Elie and St Monans, five working settlements that draw summer visitors in search of some of Scotland's choicest fish and seafood, good golf and wide sandy beaches. The crow-stepped gables and tiled roofs of these little settlements, perhaps Scotland's most appealing vernacular architecture, are an inheritance of medieval trading links with the Low Countries. The old houses range from tiny cottages lining the cobbled streets that run down to the harbours to grander merchants' houses. One of these, on the harbour front in Anstruther, houses the Scottish Fisheries Museum.

LEFT *Lobsters, crabs and crayfish decorate a house in Crail. The East Neuk is noted for the excellent shellfish caught off the rocky coastline*

Culross

There's more history further up the Firth of Forth at Culross, the best-preserved 17th-century town in Scotland and once a major port with strong links to the Low Countries, as well as an early coal-mining centre.

This picturesque settlement, set right at the water's edge, has been beautifully restored by the National Trust for Scotland and is noted for its Dutch-influenced crow-stepped houses, cobbled streets with quaint names such as Stinking Wynd and Back Causeway, and above all, for Culross Palace. It's not a royal palace, but gets its name from the Latin word *palatium*, meaning hall, and was built in the 16th century by a rich coal merchant named George Bruce. Inside, the mansion is a warren of panelled and painted small rooms and passages. Its dormer windows overlook a walled court, charmingly planted with a variety of historic species.

BELOW *Before they are painted, the walls of the houses in Culross are covered in a mix of fine gravel and cement, a process known as harling*

ABOVE LEFT AND RIGHT *The carefully preserved historic buildings in Culross are variously whitewashed or colour-washed, and roofed with red pantiles. Many have distinctive crow-stepped gables*

LEFT *This funicular railway, Britain's highest, takes visitors up to a point near the summit of Cairngorm Mountain, which by virtue of its height and position has a near-Arctic climate*

BELOW *Described by Queen Victoria as 'my dear paradise in the Highlands' Balmoral Castle has been a favourite summer residence of the Royal Family for over 150 years*

Royal Deeside and the Cairngorms

On its journey from the Cairngorms to the North Sea, the River Dee passes through an area of heather moors and lush woodlands, as well as some impressive castles. It was near the banks of the Dee in 1848, that Queen Victoria and her husband Albert began the area's royal associations when they acquired Balmoral Castle and rebuilt a grand Scottish Baronial edifice. The Royal Family still spend much time here, and attend Sunday services near by at Crathie Kirk. Above Balmoral looms the peak of Lochnagar which featured in the children's book *The Old Man of Lochnagar*, written by Prince Charles.

At the Cairngorms end, the river cascades into the Linn o' Dee, beautifully set among trees. Close by, Braemar is a bustling village with an impressive L-plan castle and home to the celebrated Braemar Gathering in early September. Further downstream, Ballater dates from the late 18th century as a spa and now thrives as a mountain resort. At Banchory salmon leap up the rapids from the Bridge of Feugh, while not far away are Castle Fraser, a fine example of the Scottish baronial style, Crathes Castle, celebrated for its highly decorative ceilings and supposedly haunted by a 'green lady', and Drum Castle where the 13th-century tower is the oldest intact structure of its kind in Scotland.

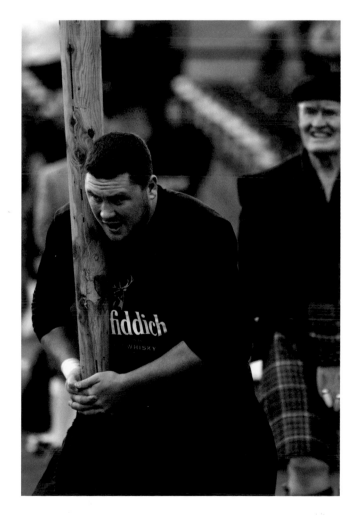

ABOVE *The Cairngorms National Park is a huge wilderness with exhilarating high-level views and challenging walks. Patches of snow often last on the mountain tops into summer*

LEFT *The Braemar Gathering and Highland Games in September has been attended by royalty ever since 1848, and features events such as tossing the caber and throwing the hammer*

Around Glen Coe

Reached from the south across the desolate wilderness of Rannoch Moor, Glen Coe is shadowed by the mighty mountains of the Three Sisters. Scotland's most dramatic glen, it runs down to the sea at Loch Leven on Scotland's west coast. This spectacular mountain valley is enclosed between conical and rugged peaks, whose slopes, cascading with rock and scree, offer some of the country's most challenging rock and ice mountaineering.

The glen's atmosphere stems partly from its sheer physical presence, but also from its place in history as the site of the notorious 1692 massacre. Backed by the Hanoverian government, the Campbells, who had been quartered with the unruly MacDonalds, violated all rules

ABOVE *A column at Glenfinnan marks where in 1745 Charles Edward Stuart – Bonnie Prince Charlie – judged he had enough support to mount a rebellion and raised his standard*

RIGHT *Regular steam services in summer run along the scenic West Highland Line from Fort William to Mallaig, crossing the Glenfinnan Viaduct, completed in 1901*

LEFT *The Three Sisters attract climbers and mountain-walkers to Glen Coe. Close by is the Lost Valley, where the Clan MacDonald hid cattle stolen from the Campbells*

of traditional Highland hospitality by slaughtering 40 of the Jacobite clan, sending the rest fleeing into a blizzard.

There are more Jacobite connections further northwest in Moidart, at Glenfinnan. This is where, in 1745, Prince Charles Edward Stuart raised his standard and gathered the clans at the start of his abortive uprising – a rebellion which was to end on the battlefield of Culloden and signal the final destruction of the Jacobite cause.

The Western Isles

Across the stormy waters of the Minch, to the west of Skye, lies the windswept string of islands of the Outer Hebrides, or Western Isles. The archipelago, 130 miles (209km) long, runs from Lewis and Harris in the north, strongholds of the sternest form of Calvinism, to Catholic Uist and Barra in the south.

This is the Gaelic-speaking edge of Britain, an elemental land where the seas smash on huge cliffs or lap against sweeping white-sand beaches. It's home to crofters, fishermen and weavers, most of whom live in the townships scattered throughout the islands and combine crofting – a unique form of land tenure and farming – with other locally based work.

Scenically, the islands are immensely different, ranging from barren peat moorland on Lewis through the bare peaks of Harris (separated only by its name) to the low-lying southern islands across the Sound of Harris. These – North Uist, Benbecula, South Uist and tiny Barra – have vast sandy beaches backed by a particularly Hebridean habitat known as machair – a flowering, grassy strand that's home to some of Britain's shyest birds.

The small town of Stornoway on Lewis is the capital, with two-thirds of the Western Isles' population living to the northwest of here in a string of close-knit crofting communities on the Nis peninsula. Many are weavers,

producing the hard-wearing and beautiful tweed that made Harris famous. Production is now centred on the largest island of Lewis.

South of Nis is the stone circle of Calanais, a mysterious structure of nearly 50 stone monoliths dating to between 3000 and 1000BC. It is one of the most important prehistoric sites in Britain.

To the south of Harris, the islands of North Uist, Benbecula and South Uist are linked by causeways, with access to Barra by ferry. From their western shores, a clear day brings views to remote St Kilda.

RIGHT *In these treeless islands, peat has always been the traditional fuel. Dug from the peat bogs during summer, it is stacked and dried for winter burning*

BELOW *Crofters once lived alongside their animals in these low, primitive dwellings, known as black houses from their smoke-blackened interiors – among other things, modernisation has brought chimneys and windows to this example*

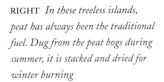

ABOVE *This meticulous re-creation of an Iron Age round house at Bosta on the Isle of Lewis stands where archaeologists unearthed a Norse settlement built over earlier houses*

RIGHT *The stone circle of Calanais is made from the local Lewis gneiss; the tallest stone marks the entrance to a burial chamber*

155

Isle of Skye

Skye derives its name from the Norse *ski*, meaning 'misty isle', and nothing could be more apt for this stunning island, the largest of the Inner Hebrides. Its mountains, often veiled in mist or wreathed in cloud, were formed by intense volcanic activity and glacial erosion, making its landscape among the most impressive in Britain. This is seen at its spectacular best in the Cuillins, jagged and menacing mountains to the west, but there's more drama

ABOVE *Neist Point Lighthouse marks the most westerly point in Skye and makes an excellent vantage point for spotting whales, dolphins, porpoises and basking sharks*

RIGHT *The monument to Jacobite heroine Flora MacDonald – who helped Bonnie Prince Charlie to escape after Culloden – in the cemetery at Kilmuir. Thousands attended her funeral in 1790*

in Trotternish to the north, where craggy rock formations, formed of residual basalt, rise up in the eerie landscape of the Quiraing, a landscape formed from landslip.

Skye was annexed by Norway in the 8th century and later blighted by the Clearances, when the local clans were cleared to make way for the more profitable sheep. In the 19th century, thousands sailed to the New World, and their descendants still return to seek their roots in places such as

Dunvegan, a 15th-century castle and seat of the Macleods, and the crofting townships around Portree. This is the island's capital, a snug fishing harbour, lined with colour-washed houses, on the east coast.

From here, the road runs southeast to Kyleakin and the road bridge that now links Skye with the mainland.

BELOW *The eastern coast of the Trotternish peninsula has extraordinary, almost lunar rock formations, including the Old Man of Storr and the Quiraing*

Index

Page numbers in *italic* refer to photographs

Acknowledgements

The Automobile Association would like to thank the following photographers, companies and picture libraries for their assistance in the preparation of this book.

Abbreviations for the picture credits are as follows – (t) top; (b) bottom; (c) centre; (l) left; (r) right; (AA) AA World Travel Library.

1 Graham Oliver/Alamy; 2 Stephen Emerson/Alamy; 3 AA/G Edwardes; 4/5 Keith Morris/Alamy; 8-9 Jon Arnold Images Ltd/Alamy; 10-11 AA/J Tims; 11 Banana Pancake/Alamy; 12 AA/J Tims; 12/13 AA/R Strange; 14 AA/C Sawyer; 15t AA/J Tims; 15b AA/J Tims; 16 AA/J Tims; 16/17 AA/N Setchfield; 17t AA/N Setchfield; 17b AA/J Tims; 18 AA/J Tims; 18/19 AA/S Montgomery; 20/21 AA/A Burton; 22 Photolibrary Group; 23 Photolibrary Group; 24/25 AA/M Busselle; 25t Peter Barritt/Alamy; 25b David Ball/Alamy; 26 Stuart Wilson/Getty Images; 27t Alan Crowhurst/Getty Images; 27b Eamonn McCormack/WireImage; 28 Photolibrary Group; 29t Photolibrary Group; 29b Roy Rainford/Robert Harding; 30 AA/J Miller; 31t AA/M Moody; 31b AA/M Moody; 32/33 AA/J Miller; 33 AA/J Miller; 34 AA/D Croucher; 34/35 AA/A Burton; 35 AA/S & O Mathews; 36 AA/W Voysey; 37 Les Gibbon/Alamy; 38 copyright of the Dean and Canons of Windsor; 39t AA/J Tims; 39b AA/J Tims; 40/41 AA/A Burton; 42/43 AA/E Meacher; 43 AA/M Moody; 44 James Osmond Photography/Alamy; 45l NobleImages/Alamy; 45r Andrew Duke/Alamy; 46t AA/M Jourdan; 46/47 Stephen Emerson/Alamy; 47 AA/A Burton; 48 AA/E Meacher; 48/49b I Capture Photography/Alamy; 48/49t Cotswolds Photo Library/Alamy; 49 I Capture Photography/Alamy; 50/51 AA/A Burton; 51t Derek Stone/Alamy; 51b AA/A Burton; 52 Elly Godfroy/Alamy; 52/53 ICP/Alamy; 53 AA/C Jones; 54 Greg Balfour Evans/Alamy; 55t David Crosbie/Alamy; 55b John Arnaud/Alamy; 56t AA/G Edwardes; 56b AA/P Baker; 57 AA/G Edwardes; 58/59 AA/G Edwardes; 60 AA/A Burton; 61l David Cunningham/Alamy; 61r AA/C Jones; 62t Peter Barritt/Alamy; 62b AA/J Wood; 63 Paul Melling/Alamy; 64/65 AA/S Lewis; 66tl Jeff Morgan 11/Alamy; 66tr Joan Gravell/Alamy; 66b The Photolibrary Wales/Alamy; 67 AA/M Moody; 68 Sebastian Wasek/Alamy; 68/69 Adam Burton/Alamy; 70/71 Adam Burton/Alamy; 71t Peter de Clercq/Alamy; 71b Simon Tilley/Alamy; 72 nagelestock.com/Alamy; 72/73 Peter Barritt/Alamy; 73 AA/R Coulam; 74 John Davidson/Alamy; 74/75 George Standen/Alamy; 76 AA/S Lewis; 77 Philip Smith/Alamy; 78 AA/S Lewis; 78/79 Keith Morris/Alamy; 79 Ian Nellist/Alamy; 80/81 Alan Novelli/Alamy; 81 George Brice/Alamy; 82t AA/N Jenkins; 82b Holmes Garden Photos/Alamy; 83 Holmes Garden Photos/Alamy; 84t AA/Mark Bauer; 84c AA/Mark Bauer; 84/85 John Warburton-Lee Photography/Alamy; 86/87 Photolibrary Group; 88t AA/M Morris; 88b AA/C Jones; 88/89 John Bentley/Alamy; 90 Imagebroker/Alamy; 91tl CW Images/Alamy; 91tr Richard Zanettacci/Alamy; 91b Imagebroker/Alamy; 92/93 Imagebroker/Alamy; 93 Craig Holmes Premium/Alamy; 94/95 Travelbild.com/Alamy; 95t Graham Harrison/Alamy; 95b David Jones/Alamy; 96 Ivor Clarke/Alamy; 97 James Osmond Photography/Alamy; 98 Archimage/Alamy; 98/99 Jon Bower Cambridge/Alamy; 99 AA/M Moody; 100t AA/N Setchfield; 100b Dave Porter/Alamy; 101tl AA/N Setchfield; 101tr AA/T Mackie; 101b Dave Porter/Alamy; 102/103 Sid Frisby/Alamy; 103t Sid Frisby/Alamy; 103b Greg Balfour Evans/Alamy; 104/105 Chris Herring/Alamy; 104l AA/T Mackie; 104r AA/T Mackie; 105 AA/T Mackie; 106t AA/T Mackie; 106b Robert Estall Photo Agency/Alamy; 107 Stuart Aylmer/Alamy; 108/109 Eli Pascall-Willis/Alamy; 110 AA/T Mackie; 111l AA/T Mackie; 111r Robbie Shone/Alamy; 112t Gary Stones/Alamy; 112cl AA/T Mackie; 112br AA/J Beazley; 112/113 AA/T Mackie; 114/115 AA/D Clapp; 115t AA/D Clapp; 115b AA/D Clapp; 116 AA/D Tarn; 117l AA/T Mackie; 117r Gillian Moore/Alamy; 118 AA/H Williams; 119t Mike Kipling Photography/Alamy; 119bl AA/T Mackie; 119br Bon Appetit/Alamy; 120 AA/D Clapp; 121 AA/D Clapp; 122/123 AA/M Kipling; 123 AA/M Kipling; 124t AA/M Kipling; 124b AA/M Kipling; 127l Jason Friend Photography Ltd/Alamy; 127r Michelle Chaplow/Alamy; 126 John Morrison/Alamy; 127t Nick Bodle/Alamy; 127b Keith Taylor/Alamy; 128/129 Lee Frost/Robert Harding; 129 David Robertson/Alamy; 130/131 AA/R Coulam; 131t Richard Sharrocks/Alamy; 131b AA/R Coulam; 132/133 Doug Houghton/Alamy; 134t AA/K Blackwell; 134/135 AA/K Blackwell; 135 John McKenna/Alamy; 136/137 Neale Clark/Robert Harding; 137t AA/J Smith; 137c AA/K Blackwell; 137b AA/K Blackwell; 138 Lynne Evans/Alamy; 139tl AA/K Paterson; 139tr AA/S Anderson; 139b John Peter Photography/Alamy; 140 AA/S Gibson; 140/141 Andrew Surridge/Alamy; 141 AA/S Whitehorne; 142t Colinspics/Alamy; 142b AA/K Paterson; 143 David Robertson/Alamy; 144/145 Nick McGowan-Lowe/Alamy; 145l Kenny Williamson/Alamy; 145r AA/D W Robertson; 146t Robert Morris/Alamy; 146b David Burton/Alamy; 147 AA/R Elliott; 148t Stephen Finn/Alamy; 148b D Hale-Sutton/Alamy; 149tl David Robertson/Alamy; 149tr Doug Houghton/Alamy; 149b AA/J Smith; 150t Callum Bennetts/Alamy; 150b Shenval/Alamy; 151t Cody Duncan/Alamy; 151b Shenval/Alamy; 152/153 Derek Croucher/Alamy; 152 John Peter Photography/Alamy; 153 Blackout Concepts/Alamy; 154t Lynne Evans/Alamy; 154b Lynne Evans/Alamy; 155t ScotImage/Alamy; 155b AA/S Whitehorne; 156t Stephen Emerson/Alamy; 156b Patrick Dieudonne/Robert Harding; 156/157 Derek Croucher/Alamy

Gatefolds (in order of appearance)

Brighton: Hove Peace Statue, Nick Hawkes/Alamy; Bronze sculpture, Tony Watson/Alamy; Brighton Pavilion, Tony Watson/Alamy; Brighton Pier, Photolibrary Group; Max Miller statue, PE Forsberg/Alamy; The Lanes, Jim Holden/Alamy; station clock, AA/W Voysey

Cotswolds: Broadway, Tamara Kuzminski/Alamy; Cotswold Way, AA/S Day; Blenheim Palace, Mark Beton/UK/Alamy; Miserden, Cotswolds Photo Library/Alamy; St Lawrence's Church, G Owston (Gloucestershire)/Alamy; cheese rolling, Nick Turner/Alamy; Bibury, Beata Moore/Alamy

Lake District: Windermere, AA/A Mockford & N Bonetti; Wordsworth family grave, Stan Pritchard/Alamy; Dove Cottage, Brian Stark/Alamy; view from Skiddaw Range, Gavin Hellier/Robert Harding; Great Langdale, Tony West/Alamy; Ashness bridge, AA/T Mackie; Castlerigg stone circle, Eli Pascall-Willis/Alamy;

Mull: boat at Croig, Stuart Aylmer/Alamy; Ben More, David Burton/Alamy; Torosay Castle, Robert Morris/Alamy; otter, Photolibrary Group; Tobermory, Ian Macrae Young/Alamy; view towards Iona, Peter Barritt/Alamy; Iona Abbey, Image Source/Alamy

Every effort has been made to trace the copyright holders, and we apologise in advance for any accidental errors. We would be happy to apply any corrections in the following edition of this publication.